T0064468

PARVARISH

PARVARISH

Making children successful

JAYDEV SINH SONAGARA

PARTRIDGE
A Penguin Random House Company

Copyright © 2015 by Jaydev Sinh Sonagara.

ISBN:	Softcover	978-1-4828-5866-2
	eBook	978-1-4828-5865-5

All rights reserved. No part of this book may be used or reproduced by any means, graphic, electronic, or mechanical, including photocopying, recording, taping or by any information storage retrieval system without the written permission of the author except in the case of brief quotations embodied in critical articles and reviews.

Because of the dynamic nature of the Internet, any web addresses or links contained in this book may have changed since publication and may no longer be valid. The views expressed in this work are solely those of the author and do not necessarily reflect the views of the publisher, and the publisher hereby disclaims any responsibility for them.

Print information available on the last page.

To order additional copies of this book, contact
Partridge India
000 800 10062 62
orders.india@partridgepublishing.com

www.partridgepublishing.com/india

Contents

paravarish.com is a live contact platform for the parents. Here you will find new information, happenings that take place within the classroom, changes in the style of education, new thoughts and answer of your questions.

Keep yourself updated with the very useful content on parvarish.com
For updates, follow us on: www.paravarish.com
or
Find us on facebook: facebook.com/paravarish

Why this book has been written

My 30 years' experience in the field of education brought me to a feeling that my understanding of dealing with the children can be useful to the parents. I sincerely felt that my experience could prove helpful to the parents in understanding the behaviour of their children, accepting them and improving the family atmosphere by right upbringing of the children. My experience could also be helpful to those who have recently entered parenthood, in dealing with the shortcomings and weaknesses of their children and in solving many other problems related to child-rearing.

- This book is written with a view to acquaint people with the results that we got while experimenting in the classrooms and carrying out educational activities.
- This book is written to reveal the open secrets, efforts and element of fate that transformed the continually-failing institutions into highly successful ones.
- This book can be helpful in infusing a fresh hope in the new generation, accepting their different approaches and in delightful upbringing of the child.
- The book will be helpful in understanding that child-rearing is a gift given by god, a wealth,

a cosmos in itself, a ray of hope, an asset of life and an opportunity beyond mortal grasp. It is an alchemy that transforms a man into human.

Foreword

Education is the key factor for shaping of life. The child is born on this earth with endless possibilities. His potential blooms if right environment is given. It's like the water that flows beneath the land. The layers of soil and rocks prevent it to come out on surface. Water emerges when such obstructions are removed. It's same for upbringing of the child. Proper education removes the obstructions, giving way to his hidden potential to emerge.

On my trip to America I came across a beautiful quotation.

"Parents should be True Parents".

You don't become parents by merely giving birth to a child. You become true parents when you rightly shape your child's life.

Child-rearing can be compared to penance. Today, you get a hoard of books in market on the subject of child development, but the 'PARVARISH', penned by Jaydev sinh leaves a different mark among all of them.

Jaydevsinh Sonagara is basically a man of education, who has spent a large part of his life in the field of education and has a broad experience in this sector. He successfully manages number of schools including the Divyapath. Moreover, he also contributes greatly in the management of SGVP, Chharodi. He is a man with god-gifted talent.

He understands the problems related to the children, parents and the education field and he works hard to solve it. This book is a result of his wide experience in the education field. I am sure that this book will be proved as a source of inspiration and guidance for the parents. Parents who desire to give a beautiful shape to their child's life must read this book. They should ponder over its content and should apply it in their life.

'Parvarish' is a Farsi word which nearly means "to take care", "to rear" or "to nurture". Child-rearing is not about providing the child with good clothes, nutritional food and buying him his desired stuffs. Child-rearing means all-round development of the child. The title of this book truly contains the essence of its content. I congratulate Jaydevsinh Sonagara for writing this inspirational book.

Swami Madhavpriyadasji
Shri Swaminarayan Gurukul,
SGVP Chharodi.

Dt: 09-08-2011
Putrada Ekadashi

Listen, what the child says

The child says:

Don't show me the way,
I walk on your steps.

I don't want your help in all matters,
let me struggle to learn new things myself.

Don't compare me with others,
I am unique in this world.

Don't advise me in all matters,
I too understand things.

I ask questions, not to get information,
but to satisfy my own curiosity.

I am not so stupid who disregard your good counsels.
In fact I test you how good you are in persuading me.

Encourage me,
and I'll never discourage you.

When I fail at learning,
please don't lose patience, please keep trying.

I am not so impudent who disrespect your instructions.
In fact I test your patience and tolerance.

I don't need dreams but the confidence on myself,
which as my parents only you can give me.

Don't hide life's truths from me,
as I too have to confront them one day.

When failure strikes me,
what I need is not your counsels but encouragement.

I have come to existence, not to
become a doctor or engineer,
but to be a good human being.

I am not a device to fulfill your expectations,
but mere a medium to carry life together.

I understand your pain,
wish you too can read my emotions.

School is not meant to shape my goals,
but to shape my life.

Do what you want to teach me,
I will learn from your actions.

Whatever I do,
is mere reflection of your being.

I don't need facilities,
but consistency of life.

I too will succeed one day,
don't put me on trial day-to-day.

Where is me in this vain complexity?

I am the focal point of my family. I am the dream of my family. I am the fulfillment of wedding vows and actualization of parents' love. I am the dawn of my family's hope. I am the hubbub in the drawing room, a wonderful blend of array and disarray.

Mamma, I am the glow of your eyes. I am the one who peep through your dimples. I am the damp on your eyelash and sweet smile on your lips. I am the beauty twirling with your hairs. I am the love that twinkles in your lap. I am the gravity of your familial bonds.

Papa, I am the motive behind your sweat. I am the centre of all of your planning. I am the spring of your commitment and essence of your toil. I am the one who keeps you busy in whole life.

I am the one who, the people say, continue the lineage. I am the one whom the society calls vision. I am the string of hope that unites the society. I am the pleasant dance and reverberating applause on the societal stage. I am the tunes of their sacred hymns and a treasure of abundant merrymaking. I am the tender beam of the societal light.

I am a scapegoat sent to the wilderness of the classroom. I am the dumb who put up with incessant discourses of the teacher. I am the philosopher's stone that actualizes their dreams. I am the mirror of their ideals. I am the drudge who bears the load of teacher's knowledge and a means to transmit it. I am the nectar of teacher's self-worth.

I am the carrier of school's life. I am its will to last. I am the grandeur of its inner music, one for whom all the prizes are contrived. I am the mark of equality and the reflection of school's past. I am the stairway swiftly leading the school to the realm of repute.

Though I seem to be on the top of the world, I am helpless and downhearted. I am the way out from this confusing tangle and yet looked upon as a culprit. I am the ashes of the incomplete smile. I am the innocent one who follows your instructions, one who laughs when you laugh, even though I am being scolded, insulted or beaten by you. Though this entire system is set up around me, my voice is heard nowhere amid these concrete jungles. Then, where is me in this vain complexity?

Reap as you sow

Our society is on the verge of a change. A kind of narrowness in relationships is seen in the affluent families. A family having meal together has become a rare sight, except for the dining table of a restaurant. People, who are eager in keeping up-to-date information about the families of Amitabh Bachchan or Bill Gates, are found miles away from the matters of their own family. A father who has reached the summit of Himalaya fails to reach to the heart of his child.

The relationship between the parents and children seem like a matter of past amongst the growing number of old-age homes. Children turning away face from their parents in search of love and affection from somewhere else tell the story of failed families. Then, you also have a hoard of people trying to take undue advantage of the atmosphere of bitter relationships among your family members. That is why I feel it is necessary for the parents to understand the importance of being guardian and companion of their children and keeping warm relationship with them.

The parents who have sacrificed their night's sleep for their children many a time put on stake their relationship with their children for an issue of mere five to ten minutes. The parents who can readily squander their entire wealth for their children often muddle their relationship over the account of hardly a hundred bucks. Parents, who walk miles for their children, avoid taking a couple of steps with them and rather become desperate to move away from them. The parents who sacrifice their day's meal for children create squabbles over a toffee or ice-cream. The parents, who feel no fatigue in praising their children, boil their blood for the matter of few marks in exams.

We see children avert the presence of their parents and resort to their friends to share their feelings, children who alter their own mark-sheets, children who veil the complaints the school made against them, children who await freedom in order to express their likes and dislikes, and children who rather prefer to seclude than to greet their father on his homecoming. I feel the parents of these children should change their approach and must find-out the reasons for how are they responsible for such situations?

If parents find no hesitation in lying, the children too will learn to speak lie.

Beating the child makes him shameless. To make him to do work by temptation makes him greedy. Preventing him to do work on his own makes him timid. Pampering makes the child stubborn. Giving him too much freedom makes him willful. Threatening him for curbing his bad habits makes him rigid.

His self-confidence diminishes when he is not appreciated for his good deeds. A few encouraging words for his good work makes his strength bloom like anything. He does his work happily when a peaceful atmosphere is kept in the house.

If parents take interest in philanthropic activities, the child too develops inclination for charity. When child is given respect during conversation, he cultivates self-respect. If a child is taught the language of love, he learns to talk gently with others. Teasing him in front of others, he develops inferiority complex for himself.

If parents take refuge in lying before the child, he imitates them and develops a habit of lying. If parents do all the works which the child should do, either because of lack of confidence on his abilities or out of too much of love, the child remains dependent on others throughout his life.

The children whose parents remain too busy and find no time for them, becomes bad-tempered. If a child needs something but denied by the parents, he is induced to steal. If parents give respect to their elders, the child too learns giving respect. When the child is dealt with rudeness, he in turn becomes impolite.

Be a child while dealing with your child and you create an intimate bond with him. Tell instructive stories to him and his creativity will increase. But raise him in distressful atmosphere in the house and he will develop a tendency of quarreling. Use insulting words and you will obstruct his growth. Give him a lavish hand in using money and he will disregard the value of money, becoming recklessly wasteful.

When the children are treated with comforting behaviour, they learn keeping calm. When the children are reared in a loving atmosphere, they grow into affectionate human beings. When they are treated with unjust behavior, they become bad-tempered.

When parents keep moderation in their lifestyle, the child in turn learns discipline. When family members keep respect for each other, the child too learns becoming humble. When the child is taken to temple regularly, he develops a religious spirit in himself. When the child sees orderliness in the life of his parents, he too develops liking for orderliness. When the child is reared in the closeness of nature – mountains, rivers, trees – he develops a comprehensive vision and become fond of natural life. When the child sees his parents feeding animals, he grows compassion for animals from his early age. If parents show hospitality towards the guests, the child also becomes courteous.

It is we, the parents, who need to change our attitudes to strengthen our relationship with the children, even in the midst of difficult situations. We need to learn that we can use tolerance as cement, good feelings as sand, and sensibility as water to strengthen the foundation of our relationship with the child.

When can the child-rearing be a process of natural joy?

- When the parents understand their child well.
- When the parents restrain their own expectations.
- When the parents try to adjust themselves with the child.
- When the parents can give quality time to the child.
- When the parents recognize the hidden potential of their child.
- When the parents provide development opportunities to the child.
- When the parents treat their child without any preconception and prejudice.
- When the parents stand beside their child during his failures.
- When the parents listen to what their child wants to say.
- When the parents tactfully rectify the bad habits and shortcomings of their child.
- When the parents do not gauge their child only through his exam results.
- When the parents become child-like while being with their child.
- When the parents can reach to the heart of their child.
- When the parents be a role model for their child instead of a preacher.

- When the parents understand the measures of growth linked with the child's age.
- When the parents cultivate inexhaustible patience in themselves.
- When the parents stop comparing their child with other children.
- When the parents be ready to bring change in themselves.
- When the parents can embrace the new thoughts and methods of child-rearing.

Child-rearing becomes a process of natural joy, instead of a burden, when the parents take their child as a gift of God, a form of God.

Academic education is not enough for the full realization of the child's potential. The responsibility of developing his body, mind, interests, inclinations, arts, hobbies, imagination, health and a vision to look at the world is far greater than merely providing him with schooling.

Above all is teaching him values, which can be inculcated not through teaching, but the child learns it automatically from the behavior and the way of living of his parents.

'Catch them young' is the principle that you should remember while edifying your child. Things that are observed, experienced, understood and accepted during the early years of 3 to 12 remain with the child throughout his life, but once he crosses the age 12 it becomes too difficult to instill good habits and values in him.

The innocent mind under the age 12 accepts and learns things out of sheer trust on the elders. But after crossing this age, he does not allow things to enter so easily into his mind. He learns to evaluate things with his logic before accepting them; hence it becomes difficult to teach him anything after this age.

Child development milestones: Age 3-4

Physical	Mental	Linguistic	Emotional	Social
Can paddle big toys and play with them.	Can hold pencil through both hands.	Can hear and respond accordingly.	Can express different emotions.	Can learn habit of going toilet himself.
Can pull toys tied with rope.	Can arrange simple stuffs.	Can speak names.	Likes to play with toys wrapped in cloths.	Can copy somebody's behavior.
Can run for a little and can kick things through his legs.	Can turn the book pages and identify the pictures inside it.	Can understand simple instructions.	Have curiosity to see and use things. Doesn't know fear.	Likes to copy household activities.
Can climb up and down on simple staircase.	Can build about six tower cubes.	Can speak his name.	Always try to attracting attention towards him.	Can use dining tools on watching others doing it.
Can climb the stairs using the railing.	Can draw simple geometric shapes.	Can speak the names of body parts and show them.	Can understand appreciation.	Can play tricks to grab the attention of his parents.

Child development milestones: Age 4-5

Physical	Mental	Linguistic	Emotional	Social
Can stand on one foot for a while.	Can identify colours and speak its names.	Can ask questions.	Can understand the emotional ties between the members of his family.	Mixes with other members of the house.
Can use necessary tools when going out of house.	Can make logical arrangement of toys.	Can speak name, age and address.	Get rid of the habit of bedwetting	Can mix with other children in the school.
Can stably run on his legs, can jump.	Can complete drawings using pencil colours.	Can speak and count numbers from 1 to 10.	Wants to take part in household activities.	Can develop cleanliness using fork and knife.
Can run through small hurdles.	Can use children's scissors.	Can give answers using sentences.	Develops liking-disliking for people and places.	Likes to share food with others.
Can ride three-wheeled cycle on the street.	Can hold the pencil properly.	Can converse with others.	Starts having feelings of faith and doubt.	Likes to draw pictures and play toys.
Can kick the ball in particular direction.	Can give curves to his handwritings.	Likes to listen his favorite stories again and again.	Starts having sense of experiences of past and present.	Develops awareness of going toilet himself, and of the time and place.

Child development milestones: Age 5-6

Physical	Mental	Linguistic	Emotional	Social
Can dance along with music.	Can draw landscapes and fill colours.	Eager to learn new words.	Have control over what he wants to express.	Develops imagination power.
Can play all games using ball.	Can use tools to draw shapes.	Can talk about characters of the stories while showing expressions.	Learns to take care of his younger siblings.	Learns to use things like knife.
Can keep balance.	Can draw figures giving it clean shape. Have a sense of proportion in the drawing.	Gives his introduction, celebrates his birthday.	Help friends, understands their feelings.	Put together toys logically.
Can jump and play games like *langadi*.	Develops understanding into numbers and calculation.	Can remember songs.	Make friends and be with them while keeping distance with others.	Develops a sense of sharing things.
Can keep balance while walking through narrow spaces.	Can draw proportionately the shapes of door-window.	Likes to hear jokes and funny stories.	Likes to jest, play prank.	Likes to stay clean. Likes appreciation.
Can hang with his hand and maintain grip.	Can use pen, pencil, crayon and differentiate between various kind of papers.	Able to read, write and speak language.	Makes group of friends in the class. Feels liking-disliking.	Learns to wash hands-legs himself.

These tables are meant for just giving you an overall idea about how the child grows over a period of time. It is not based on any hard-and-fast scientific facts.

Mothers should not assess their child by this table. You will find some children doing batter on one or other front, while there will be some who are lagging behind in some area.

A child's growth should be figured out by looking at his Intelligence Quotient, Emotional Quotient and also by his Social Quotient. Never assess him merely by his exam results.

Besides, the child learns a few things speedily or slowly depending upon his familial atmosphere.

In India, you see children having strong social and emotional quotients. Japan is ahead in skill-based growth. Children in America are ahead in learning manners. Children of poor or developing countries do batter when it comes to working hard. Children in Russian countries develop good affinity with nature, while African countries have much liking for music. Children in Muslim countries are firmer in observing religious and social customs, while those living in islands develop more love for the sea and ecology.

One needs to understand this diversity in order to fathom the grandeurs of mother earth and the atmosphere that surrounds it.

When you look at a place in its entirety, you find many interesting things. For example, Rajasthan has an interesting geography, geography contains history, history has math in it, math contains life, and life is a divine creation of God himself, which finds its most beautiful expression in childhood. Therefore, the childhood is a phenomenon that must be understood well.

When you look India from top, you find tall and healthy people in Punjab-Haryana. They are light-brown-skinned and beautiful. Move towards south and the height starts decreasing, belly increasing and skin colour getting darken. In south, people have strong intellect and professional skills. Gujarat falls in the middle of north and south India and so Gujarati people have mix traits of both these ends.

The north India has faced many foreign attacks and so the people residing there are more aggressive, opposing, combative and rebellious, while even today the people in south are relatively calm.

People of Punjab-Haryana get into military as they have strong physique, while people in south take competitive exams, become IAS officers and take charge as their bosses. Gujarati people get into business, sell things to both of them, and earn wealth.

Challenges ahead

Usually while enrolling their children in the school the parents keeps contemporary scenario in mind. They consider aspects like choosing the English or Gujarati medium school, the opportunities and environment provided to the children in the school.

However, there is one important aspect related to child development which the parents and the school organizers either do not understand or have no clue about it. The point is that when the child comes out in the world after 25 years of education, the world is completely different than it was 25 years back. He has to face a completely different set of circumstances, a completely different set of problems.

Some 25 years back it was common for class-5-schoolers to not regularly attending the school. It was a major concern for the parents. Also the children were not refined in the use of language and like to roam around instead of staying at home.

15 years back the scenario was different. The children used to dislike ordinary school bags. They wanted attractive shoes, clothes and latest compass box. The children were quite concerned about their image. They used to demand scooter instead of cycle for going to school.

Five years back the children started demanding car to take them to school. Now they wanted mobile phones and other gadgets. Their school has to be of a modern style. The teachers must come by car, and all such things. Their attire, eating and outing habits, everything has completely changed.

Today in cities, almost 40% of class-5 students studying in good schools regularly use computer. They are quite familiar with the Facebook, chatting and internet, and know more in compare to their age. They watch video clips without hesitation which even adults hesitate to watch. The parents are unaware of such activities as these issues were nonexistent during their times.

The goals of the child keep changing during his life. His short-term and long-term expectations also keep changing. The parents, the teacher and the principal can be helpful to the child in setting high goals of his life.

Once there was a child who used to go school on a chariot. One day his father asked, "What do you want to become in life?" The child replied innocently, "I want to become a charioteer." The child replied so, as while going to school he had seen the charioteer controlling the horses. And in his mind the charioteer was the most commanding man among all the people he had met. His answer put his parents into a dilemma. They consulted his school principal. The principal promised to visit their house on the child's birthday. On his birthday the principal reached his home with two different gift boxes. One box had a replica of a simple chariot, while the other had the replica of lord Krishna's chariot having seven horses. The child was asked which chariot he wanted. The child replied he wanted the chariot having seven horses. They exhorted the child that if he wanted the chariot having seven horses he had to be like Krishna and Arjuna and pass through the tough tests of life. This changed entire viewpoint of the child. Now the same chariot in which he used to go to school started seeming insignificant to him. He became desperate in attaining high goals of his life. As the time passed the same child became known as a successful ruler, administrator and a visionary. Today we know him as Sayajirao Giakwad.

Society, from the perspective of child development

Successful Society	Unsuccessful Society
A successful society has a long-term vision and does its planning keeping in view the requirements of next hundred years. New generation is always the central point of its planning.	An unsuccessful society plans only to tackle present-day situations. Contemporary issues are the central point in such planning.
New generation is always given opportunities in a successful social setup.	An unsuccessful society gives importance to older generation.
Successful society uses its strengths for empowering the education system.	Unsuccessful society uses its energies for finding way out from the twists and turns of the society.
Successful society cares to spare some playing space for children among the dense array of concrete buildings.	Unsuccessful society erects concrete jungles and leaves the child suffocating in it.
A successful society is always ready in inculcating values, knowledge and information into the young generation.	Unsuccessful society teaches its customs and traditions to the new generation.
In a successful society, even an ordinary person could remain certain and unworried that his child will get enough opportunities.	In an unsuccessful society the parents remain scared and worried that their child's rights will be snatched.

A successful society is a preacher and propagator of all-round development and high values.	Unsuccessful society is ahead in bragging about its achievements, material wealth and the child's exam results.
A successful society is the one that can teach socialization, simplicity, politeness and patience to the children in a gentle manner.	Although it appears that more jobs and money is created for the young generation, the unsuccessful society, in fact, creates a horde of old-age houses and an atmosphere of insensibility.
A successful society tries to find the child in the graph of success.	An unsuccessful society tries to find a graph of success in the child.
A successful society respects the changing time and alters its customs, traditions and values accordingly, so that the young generation doesn't feel inconvenience in adopting them.	An unsuccessful society sticks with the old customs, traditions and values. It also rigidly pushes the new generation to follow them.
Successful society rejoices in observing ethics. It values and teaches the value of honesty, simplicity and fidelity to the children.	Unsuccessful society rejoices in pretentious pomp and show of performance and indirectly teaches the children worthless competing with each other.
A successful society donates to the schools with a view to nurture the academic ecology to empower the new generation.	An unsuccessful society pollutes the social atmosphere by giving extravagant alms in religious activities.
A successful society facilitates the talents, skills, interests and hobbies of all the children.	An unsuccessful society cares only for encouraging successful children, while hurtfully treats those who fail.

A successful society understands the affliction of the ordinary families, stands beside their children and helps them to succeed.	An unsuccessful society supports the children of only affluent families and lifts them to the influential stage of the society.

A Right Age for Schooling

What is the right age for a child to start schooling?

I think, a child having completed three-years of age on or before 30-6 (June 30) at the beginning of an academic year of the school can be admitted at the Nursery Level. However, in few cases the children completing 3-years on or before 30-9 (September 30) could also be given admission, provided they have good physical and mental growth.

But, because being younger in the age such children are facing stiffer competition from others in the class and finding it like an uphill task. Some parents even make phony Birthday Certificate for their child to start schooling at an early age, however, this trick could be proven counter-productive in some cases.

In fact, the smart and educated parents should take the admission of their child at one-year later age as it would ultimately benefit the child, I think.

The Nursery Schooling offers various different opportunities to the child such as – to accustom himself to spend time away from parents, particularly from mother, to develop good habits, time-management, and to do every job on his own to make him self-dependent and confident. The Nursery schooling is not for educating the child, but, to give him/her an impression that it is a system devised for him to spend joyful hours, on daily basis.

The child can be kept busy with such activities that develop his/her skills, talents and other abilities, particularly the skills that enhance the abilities of his/her fingers and eyes.

The Nursery Schooling is a system that educates the child about colours, games, shapes, toys, arrangements, neatness, food, discipline, friendship, social adaptation, freedom, fun, and self-management and so on. The school should train the nursery children in the same purview.

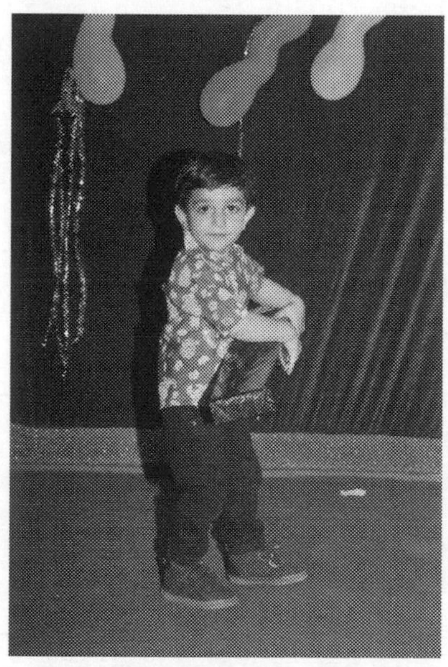

The child taking admission directly at Jr. K. G. level is not lagging behind in the education. Play School and Nursery School are arrangements for the working couples or parents having hectic life styles or having no option but to keep the child busy in the good activities.

Normally, parents make lots of experiments with the first child because of their over-enthusiasm. But, the maturity earned from these experiments is surely benefiting the second child of the family.

The child placed in the school at an early age is often facing difficulties or lag behind in the education because of his inability to grasp quickly compared to other older children.

Choosing of school, a confusion

Gujarat is witnessing vibrancy nowadays in the field of education. The State is emerging as India's hub for global education having Ahmedabad as its knowledge capital.

Parents in Gujarat, particularly in urban areas, are facing dilemma in choosing school for their little ones. The increasing hunger for education, competition and multidimensional schooling system has compelled parents to think about this question as soon as the child turns two. Before I say about the kind of school you should choose, it is important to understand different kind of affiliations and modules that schools have. About 90% of schools in Gujarat function with the certification of GSEB (Gujarat State Education Board). The GSEB syllabuses have been designed keeping in view the Gujarat's geographical condition, the interests and requirements of the Gujarati children and that of the State itself. The other is CBSE (Central Board Secondary Education) schools which have national level syllabuses with a view to facilitate the Central government employees having inter-state transferable jobs. These syllabuses have been designed keeping in mind the competitive exams taken by national-level institutes and the quality of employment and career. Gradually these syllabuses have been adopted in every state of the country.

Majority of the schools teaching with Indian Certificate for School Education (ICSE) syllabus have adopted the concept of United Kingdom School; and many countries of the world are running the school with ICSE syllabus. In the syllabus of these schools, subjects like physics, chemistry and biology are being introduced from the upper primary standard and later years gradually the customized courses get included.

This board is using the teaching technology for educating the children, thus, its study materials, teaching-learning, classroom atmosphere, technological support, and examination system are quite different compared to the local schools. In short, in the local schools learning and examination system are largely based on memory-power. While, in ICSE schools are putting more emphasize on I.Q., logic and application. In the city, we have internationally recognized courses such as Cambridge and Edexcel run by IGCSE and managed by U. K. based board. Students studying in these affiliated schools are finding it easier to move into international schools. Beside these, in Gujarat we have schools recognized by CITA (U.S.) and IB Board which are completely following the international syllabus. These international schools are providing syllabus while the school authorities have to decide course books. For teaching these kinds of syllabuses, the school requires a completely different type of teaching staff and classroom environment.

In addition to these, the Gurukul schools, run by religious sects, are providing a very successful education option that is based on the spiritual environment. Our famous

SGVP School has given many successful students to the society who had excelled in the field of sports, science and spirituality. Gurudev Shri Madhavpriyswami and Pujya Balswami are constantly putting efforts to touch the sensitivity of the classroom to prepare the children for the competition of international level. The Rajiv Gandhi Open School, run by the Central Government, possesses a unique importance. The Ashram schools run by the governments are educating the children at very minimal cost. For the students having inclination towards ancient language of Sanskrit has an option to choose Sanskrit schools and acquire graduation degree in it.

What should you teach to a five year old child?

- A child should be taught to speak, to read and to write his name, address and telephone number.
- Teach him the name of his parents.
- The child should be aware of his residential location.
- Teach him how to wear and change his clothes.
- Teach him how to open and close his pant's zip.
- Teach him to put his stuffs at right place.
- The child should know how to behave with others.
- Child should be taught a few words of good manners and good wishes.
- He should be taught to sit properly and to get adjusted with others.
- He should be taught to get mixed and mingled with the friends.
- A child should be taught to wear shoes and tying-untying shoelace.
- He should be taught to use toilet properly.
- Make him aware about to wash hands before eating and after using toilets.
- Cultivate in him interest for learning language, music and painting.
- Teach him to give respect to his parents and elders.

Some smart kids learn a lot from their surroundings, some need to be taught, while others need to be instructed repeatedly.

Most children learn such habits and deeds by observing their family members. They also learn it from the characters of interesting stories. Parents should especially tell parables, fairytales and religious stories to them.

What should you teach to a nine year old child?

- Teach him to say 'please' before asking anything from others and 'thank you' on receiving it.
- Teach him that in case he wants to say something while two elders are talking, he should keep patience and wait till the elders complete their conversation. And if it is urgent and necessary then he should politely say 'excuse me' and then put his point in the middle of the conversation.
- Teach him to ask whenever he has a doubt or lack of self-confidence. The habit of asking can save him from many problems.
- Teach him especially that he should not make a comment in public on someone's physical appearance, language, religion and caste.
- Teach him to answer nicely when someone asks 'How are you?', and also to ask courtesy question in response.
- Teach him to say 'Thank you' for using his friends' items. He should also say 'Thank you' to the family members of his friend while leaving friend's house after playing.
- Teach your child to knock the door before entering someone's house or bedroom, and to enter only after getting a reply from the other side.

- Teach him to introduce himself before starting a conversation with someone on the phone. He should also make sure that the person on the other-end is the correct person with whom he really wants to talk.
- Teach him to shake hands with others and say 'Thank you' with a sense of gratitude upon receiving gifts or help from them.
- Stop him from using slang; teach him good words.
- See that your child doesn't call his friends or others with their teasing nicknames.
- Stop your child from jeering, mocking and laughing at someone's mistake, commenting on someone's physical limitations, on his friend's name or his family. Stop him from beating or punishing someone.
- Teach him to sit quietly at the events like prayer, meeting or sports match which are uninteresting to him. Let him know that the person on the stage is performing with the best to his capacity.
- Teach him to say 'Excuse me' whenever he needs to interrupt other's activity.
- Teach your child to cover his face with tissue while sneezing and coughing and to say 'Excuse me' after it.
- Teach him the courtesy that on passing through the door he should patiently hold the door-open for the next person walking behind him.
- Teach him to say 'May I help you?' when his elders, parents or teachers are doing some work.

- Teach him to gladly help the elders whenever they ask for it.
- Teach him dining manners, using of dining tools and keeping cleanliness.
- Teach your child a habit to keep a napkin with him while eating and to keep his mouth clean with it.
- Teach him that while on dining table he should request others to pass on the food instead of dragging it towards him.
- Teach your child to put his shoes, lunchbox, school bag and uniform at right place after returning home from school.
- It is important to teach him traffic rules for safety and how to ride bicycle on the road.
- Teach him to put his demands before his parents in the form of request.
- Teach your child to stay safe during the celebrations of Uttrayan, Holi or Diwali.
- Teach him how to sit safely on the vehicle, using the seat-belt and to be watchful for his safety while riding in the car or school van.
- Teach him the safe usage of harmful gadgets like sharpener, blade and knife.
- Teach your child to keep his shields, trophies, certificates and files in a systematic and secure manner.
- Teach him to take part in school activities, to make representation before the teacher, to solve small problems on his own and whose help should he seek while facing bigger problems?

- He must be able to understand simple English, write in cursive and at least to speak it a little.

Parents' behavior is the very first schooling for the children. It is important for parents to understand that the children learn most things not by continuous persuading but from the parents' behaviour.

What should you teach to a twelve year old child?

- Teach your child to talk candidly about his needs and problems.
- Teach him how to make request to others and how to convince them.
- If your child studies in English medium school, teach him to speak simple English and to explain things to others in English.
- Assure him that he can frankly talk about his problems with his parents.
- Teach him that things have their own prices and quality, and that he should check it before buying things.
- Teach him how to coordinate with other students of his class and represent his thoughts before his class teacher.
- Teach your class-7 studying child to read and write in his mother-tongue in a proper manner. He should develop an interest in good handwriting and good reading. This way, he will be able to express his ideas in a much better way.
- Teach your child how he can access the telephone numbers of the bank, post office, railway station, police station and fire brigade. Besides, he should know the basics of computers and internet. He must know how to get such information and how to take help of these resources when needed.

- A class-7 child should be able to dial 108 for calling an ambulance, if needed. He should know how to be safe at home when he is alone, and to contact a nearby relative when needed.
- He should know how to take care of his younger siblings, besides, being helpful to elders in their work. Perhaps he may like to help his parents when they return home from job.
- A class-7 child should be able to stitch button on his cloths, make use of needle-thread, cut vegetables and prepare tea/coffee. Teach him the use of the appliances like refrigerator, oven, gas, dishwasher etc. and maintain cleanliness in home.
- Teach him about the electrical points in house and about the electric appliances. Teach him about computer maintenance, using the TV, charging the electronic gadgets such as mobile phone.
- Teach him about the genital differences, physical changes that take place with the increased age and about the importance of keeping the body parts clean. Giving them sex education is necessary. If you hesitates to do it, or yourself unclear about it, you can find books in the market which explain this subject as per the age of your child. Keep such books at your home, child will read it.
- If there is complaint about the child's irregularity, behaviour and studies, parents should discuss it with the teachers and must try to improve the situation.

- A class-7 student should be able to take care of his shoes, cloths, tools, schoolbag etc. He should be taught to clean and dry his cloths.
- After class-7, the parents should give opportunities to the child to go on long tours, vacations and adventure camps, so that he can learn to stay away from his parents for few days.
- Parents should ensure that their child see important places and meet great people. They should encourage him to excel in the subjects of his liking and develop a broad view-point. Make good arrangements to enable him to cultivate interest in music, painting and reading.
- As the child enters the teen-age at the age of 12-13 he is passing through bodily changes and may become aggressive, depressed and too conscious about his looks and personality. Children get tensed due to the pressure of competition. This is the phase when parents should give much attention to their child.
- A book of Dr. Arati Kaswekar - '*Tarunya Sikhshan and Prajanan Swasthya*' (Adolescent education and procreation fitness) - has been read exceedingly near the girls' rest room at our school. Teenagers usually develop a kind of stubbornness and resistance and a feeling that they are right in their thinking. When you want to teach them something, teach them with patience and in a way that it does not hurt their self-respect.

- Don't scold at your teenager child in front of his younger siblings, friends and other relatives. Mostly don't give him advices in front of others.
- You get better results if you appreciate their good works and talk with them in a frank manner.

The vastness within

Every child born in this world is unique from other children. Though they apparently look same as human beings, their physical and mental traits are different. The child takes birth with certain genes; heredity from his parents, grandparents and ancestors of past few generations. Caste system is nothing but the genetic science molded for smooth carrying of human affairs. However the society has wrongly interpreted it and destroyed the very essence of it.

A child's brain has millions of cells resembling mushroom fibers. It is an incredible piece of creation by the God. Human brain's capacity to beat even the most powerful super computer points towards the existence of God. Since the people's brains are different, they have their own way of thinking and solving problems. Let's understand why so happens.

(1) Left and right brain

Human brain is a wonderful creation made up of inseparable joint cells. Its functioning is done through left and right brain. Also there is midbrain and hindbrain which controls the limbs situated in opposite direction, i.e. left brain controls the limbs of right side whereas right brain controls the limbs of the left side of the body.

Left Brain	Right Brain
(Logical) Children with active left brain are good at logic and using of logical language.	Usually the children with active right brain have inclination towards creative things and activities that need imagination viz. language, drawing, music and art.
(Sequential) They are good at sequential calculation, more accurate in guessing possible steps involved in problem solving.	Such people are bit moody when it comes to taking decision.
They are good at activities requiring intellectual skills.	People with active right brain can take successful decision even without using any sort of logic.
Active in making analysis, close examination, finding of basic constituent elements.	They are active in religious and spiritual activities and social services.
Can think in objective way, i.e. without interference of one's own feelings and thoughts.	Their ideas, opinions, way of thinking and decisions are subjective.
People with active left brain are generally right-handed. They usually have more interest in the subjects like Math and Science. People who have excelled in science field are of this type. They look situations in pieces.	Children with active right brain usually prefer to write with left hand. People who have excelled in language, art, film, writing and creativity are of this type.

With the knowledge of how the left and right brain functions, the parents can understand the way their child works. It also helps them to know the child's interests, inclinations and abilities. The parents can also decide upon certain activities which develop one or another brain of the child.

What really should you teach to your child

Parents are too zealous to teach names of birds and animals to their child. They teach him math tables, they teach him doing homework speedily and compete fiercely, but never teach what is really essential. Eventually the children who succeed in studies fail in tackling the real life. In such a situation, this article will surely prove to be very helpful in knowing what really you should teach to your child.

- Teach him to keep going when circumstances are not favourable. Children usually lose courage and succumb to failure in adverse circumstances.
- Teach him that failure is a part of success and failure is equally necessary to succeed.
- Teach him how to make good friends and then to keep them. In friendship he should know when to go ahead and when to stop.
- Teach him how to bring out his talents and seize opportunities.
- Teach him especially that simplicity, honesty, positive attitude and endurance are concrete pillars of life.
- Teach him that it is easier to earn money but difficult to save it. So, teach him how to save money and make a right use of it.

- Teach him that it is good to share his snacks, tools and toys with others and to give it those who are most needy.
- Teach him that when good times turn face from him and failures encircle him, he can still succeed the next day with persistent efforts. Teach him to cultivate such fighting spirit.
- Teach him the difference between price and value, stinging and frugality, need and desire, freedom and willfulness.
- Teach him to achieve goals with hard work instead of being sentimental about it.
- Teach him to stand with dignity when his friends or relatives ignore him or degrade him. Instead he should take the situation as a challenge.
- It is important to teach him that exams are there not only to measure your knowledge but also your ignorance. It tests not merely your knowledge but also your skills, art of representation and smartness.
- Teach him particularly how to buy things, how to check their weight and different units of measurement. Also teach him to tackle affairs at bus station, railway station, post office and bank, besides making him remember important phone numbers.
- He should know how to stay safe while alone at home. He must know the police and emergency numbers which he might need to use in case of danger. He should also know how to commute safely between the school and home.

- Teach him especially how to deal with strangers and how to remain calm and composed in the midst of accidental or god-given troubles.
- Teach him to keep his hope alive during adverse situations and have faith that he will surely get help. Parents can use inspirational stories for it.
- Parents must strive to teach their child good manners and language, habit of appreciating others, politeness, controlling anger and conversation on telephone.

To a habitually furious child his teacher once gave a hammer and a hundred nails. He asked the child to pound a nail on the tree every time he feels like angry. The child accepted the suggestion and started doing what his teacher said. Gradually his nail-beating decreased. Now the teacher asked him to remove those nails from the tree. The child did it. Teacher showed him gashes on the tree and said, "It is easy to say sorry after causing pain to someone but the scars left by the inflicted wounds on his heart can't be wiped out." The teacher's words penetrated in child so deeply that his behaviour changed completely.

Curricular and co-curricular activities

The best method to educate a child is to teach him along with some extra-curricular activities. The extra-curricular activities are developing the children's abilities to understand and giving experience too. The curricular activities help the child to develop his personality beyond boundaries drawn by the Mark-Oriented Education System. The curricular activities are providing an opportunity to every student to attain the peak in his field of interest and inclination. It is a food for mind and subconscious-mind and a vertical growth to the body's energy. It is a natural procurement. It teaches a time-management. It is the mother of personality development. It is a challenge to the Mark Based Evaluation System. It is a real education. Provide ample opportunities in curricular activities to bring out the best of him in his field of interest and inclination. Activities means a unfolding of the childhood, it means re-creation of the personality, activity means joy, activity means organizing of festivity of life, it means to convert the class-room into a heaven, activity means creation of teacher's teaching, it means sailing into the flow of education, activity means instilling the inner-self into the bundle of information, activity means experiencing the sense, it means dawn of childhood, it means to fill the eyes of child with joy and cheers, it means a natural attempt to prevent the school from becoming cemetery, activity means to rise above the books for merging into mother-nature, activity means a poetic appreciation of the school.

Activity means offering of homage to the God, it means nurturing of vision, a sheltering of interest means activity, no-string attached joy among four-walls of the class-room means activity, activity means applying of kohl in awaiting eyes, activity means flying on imagination to experience sheer joy, it means energising childhood, activity means glorifying wish over mind, activity means an attempt to convert a garden into a park, it means spreading the personality, activity means decomposition of the tension, activity means indication of arrival of nature, activity means instilling music in ear, activity means an attempt to convert knowledge, science, and yoga into an experiment, activity means transformation of teacher into a child, activity means singing of birds on veranda of the school, activity means an educative attempt to convert company into a pleasure. It must be understood that all these creations are results of the co-curricular activities, the extinction of those activities would extinct the personality. The recent reform in the education system is an initiation to convert the education into the co-education. In a chit-chat meeting with a principal of another school, after conclusion of a training programme, he opined about the training programme that "It is nothing but a plan only to pass the students in bulk at free of cost."

If the Government, Administration or System fails to change the attitude of the person concern than just like

mercury, the educated and qualified persons will be also sitting at the bottom of the lake.

The desired results could not be achieved with just an exchange of information during the training programmes organized for adaptation of a new thought, ideals or system. In fact, it is essential to give training for "ATTITUDE" change.

Factors affecting child's development

For a healthy child the first seven formative years are very important for his physical and mental growth. The child's genetic potential and learning opportunities are important elements which largely affect his mental and physical growth. By birth each baby arrives in the world with his few unique abilities of interests, inclinations and skills. But, for the further enhancements of his natural abilities it is very important that how many and what kind of opportunities and environments the parents are providing to him. Often the child having capacity and enterprising nature develops a psychological problem just because of his criticism, comparison and competitions with others. It is the responsibility of parents to provide him a healthy, a conducive, and an encouraging environment and therefore they must keep the following elements in the mind:

Physical Health:

A total Freedom to do activities, encouragements to do desired activities, a proper guidance from the parents to overcome his limitations, and healthy and hygienic homely foods make the child fit, healthy and strong.

Control over the activities, negative remarks and completely commanding the child makes him depressive. The depression makes the child angry and lazy. Sometimes too much control and sicknesses often makes the child habitually angry and pigheaded. Such children often show symptoms of stress, fear and anxiety. The children grown-up by mother with her own breast-feeding are found more healthy and energetic. These children are having higher level of adaptability to learn and accept new things.

Cheerful Environment:

It can be said, "The words **Happiness and Health** are like twins", or "A Happy child will be a healthier child too!!" The child growing-up in happiness is often found healthier. The happier child quickly develops his social relationship, attract others, and get his job done. The atmosphere filled with tension and unhappiness is resulting into diminishing the abilities of the child. Such children are developing a tendency to become negative, timid, protective and non-enterprising. The parents need to understand that rather than facilities and amenities, their attitudes, love and environments make the children happier.

Manners and Attitudes:

The positive attitude, attachment with the ground realities and setting of realistic goals make the child more successful and these elements even make the unsuccessful child to stand-up again against the difficult circumstances. It is the responsibility of the parents to give an opportunity to the talents of their child. It is better for the parents to adjust their attitudes and manners in tandem with the mould prepared by the Almighty for their child rather than imposing their own mould on him. Therefore, the interests, efforts, time and patience shown by the parents in teaching new things to the child make him successful. The parents have to make constant efforts for the child to teach him positive attitudes and making good friends.

Child's status in the Family & Competition:

Normally the first child of the family draws maximum attention, help, guidance, cooperation, and importance. Mostly these children are growing as a dependent-child. Normally, the medical attention sought by the second child of the family would not be as much as by the first-child. The struggles and attempts needed to be made by the second child for his privileges make him stubborn. Sometimes the age gap of 3-4 or more years between two children could cause more problems. Often, a noticeable vast gap appears in behavioural attitudes between the children grown-up in the joint and the satellite families. Similarly, the competitions, comparisons, and criticism between two children of the same family by its members are also affecting their personality in a very big way.

1. Security:

The children nurtured-up in the safe and secure environments are growing-up as physically healthier and mentally stubborn. These children are having more confidence, clarity in expressions, and tendency to take leadership. Compared to the children grown-up in insure and unsafe environments, the children nurtured in the safe and secure atmosphere are more focused and capable to learn, matured, and ahead in developing social relationships.

The children grown up in insecure environment, under constant negative attitude, and criticism are lacking of confidence and tend to reserve in developing new relationships. These children are falling into depression after a little failure, finding it hard to survive in struggles, and unable to utilize their genetic potentiality to full.

Beside these, other factors like children's cast, tension, relationship between mother and father, encouragements, school environment, co-education activities and the ambitions of the family are also affecting their healthy growth.

The Autistic Children

Often abnormality is observed with some children during their talks, relationships and behaviour as they are suffering from the Autism. In medical term Autism is described as "Bio-neurological disorder that is observable in early childhood with symptoms of abnormal self-absorption, characterized by lack of response or other humans and by limited ability or disinclination to communicate and socialize.

Now-a-days, the cases of children suffering from the autism are coming to limelight quickly because of awareness spreading about it in the society and availability of its medical treatments with the advancement in the medical science.

Normally, the first symptom of the autism appears in the child during the first 30-months from the birth. The child shows lack of interest or laziness in learning or following. Such children are also showing behavioural attitudes like sleeping for long-hours, less-crying and physical inactiveness. These children also start learning at later age. Sometimes parents of such children think that their child is dumb as they behave in very stereo type manners and hardly showing any facial expressions or gestures. They mostly try to avoid eye-contacts and are slow learners. Compared to girls, the Autism is prevailing 4% higher in the boys. By the age of adulthood such children are showing 30-40 % improvement, but, for that they require help, guidance and support. The child suffering from the Autism is showing intellectual growth of three-year-old at the age of 10.

If such children are not given proper care and attention than problems start arising in the daily life and family falls into a deep trouble.

The prior condition of parenting is that the Almighty put them on a test "In the form of a child" and raising a child of any form is a challenge.

A specialist doctor, a professional advisor and explicit school for Autistic children can be very helpful. The better results could be derived from the Autistic children if all of them are kept busy in the group activities like music, plays, sports, interaction and co-education. Autism is a long-term challenge and better results could be achieved with parents showing patience and tolerance than the medications.

The Children with Inability to Learn:

Often, the children starting late to speak are showing inability to learn read and write. Besides this, the problem in pronouncing words, making spellings, identifying numbers is called ***DYSLEXIA.*** The children suffering from occasional blindness are also getting trapped into this. It is mostly found in the boys and particularly children having disturbed family background.

This problem is worsening amongst the children born with the aged parents, in poverty, unemployment, physical torturing, and inadequacy of educational atmosphere, single parenting, and children living under pressure.

The children suffering from Dyslexia can be cured without medications with the help from specially trained teachers, specialised classrooms, and active parents. The Dyslexia affected children can quickly take up the challenge against the disease, if they are provided co-operation, advices and guidance by the institutions that are specifically working for such children.

Similarly, the children suffering from partial dumbness, eye-sight, grasping power can be cured quickly with positive efforts from parents and teachers than the medicines.

The Child safety at home and at school

Every year millions of children suffer from minor or major injuries due to lack of safety awareness. If the parents give a little attention to the children when they are learning to explore places in and around their house, it may save lives of millions children.

Safety at home:

Kitchen is the biggest risk-place for the children who are learning to walk. It is seen that children catch fire while coming in contact with gas or heated primus, hot plates, hot tea-coffee, cooker, toaster, oven, or while playing with the matchbox. Children are at risk of falling from the railings, balcony, platform and furniture; they are at risk of getting electric shock from different home appliances, electric socket and open cables. Chemicals, Insecticide, acid, cleaning powder, cream, liquid, cosmetics, shampoo, medicines are also dangerous for children. Glass equipments, glass bottles, knife, sharp tools and heavy items too are risky for the children. Water filled bucket, sharp-edged bucket, tubs filled with water and underground water tank are unsafe for the children. Stairs, steps and sharp stones in the home, furniture with glass corners pose danger for the children. Routine household items like scissor, needle, sharpener, and blade can be dangerous for the child. Doors and windows fixed in the wind direction can be pose danger for fingers of the children, as they might get hurt out of it. Toys like arrows, spears, and toy-guns can prove a threat to your child's safety. Fireworks, colors, beads are threat to the safety of children.

Tin container, tin drums, cupboard having quilt inside, automatic locking suitcase, automatic locking doors, and grain filled drum is dangerous for the children. Slippery floor and stairs also pose threat for the children.

Three daughters and a son of a farmer in Saurashtra lost their lives as they entered into the grain-filled drum to play. The children could not reopen the cap of the drum. Even their nails came off in the efforts, but to no avail.

Children are keen and curious to learn new things. In their impatience they might create such a big problem that we cannot imagine.

There are thousands of cases of the children swallowing or injecting things like coins, rubber, pencil, pen pieces, buttons, pulse seeds and parts of toys in their nose or mouth and get their breath stifled. We see thousands of cases of children burning their body parts on touching the silencer of bike or cut their finger in the doors of car. There are number incidents of the children falling from windows, balcony or when they climb on tables trying to look out of window. Parents should be very cautious when they go outside taking baby walker with them.

Usually children are unaware and careless about the risk to their life while crossing the road, playing in the ground or in the garden and walking in the market with elders. Out of the temptation of getting chocolate or ice-cream children can easily go along with the strangers. They even go outside alone without informing their elders to buy such stuffs if they have money with them. This approach is dangerous for the children. Travelling without wearing safety belt in van, rickshaw or in the car poses risk for the safety of a children. There are many instances of children have set on the steering wheel and started the car on their own and met with an accident.

Your pet dog, cat or street dog could cause a threat to children. Often it is seen that the child strikes or tease the pet and it attacks back on the child.

It is important that parents explain things to the children rather than frightening them. Parent should take safety measures and as far as possible children should not be left alone. Things like house furniture, bathroom, swimming pool, cupboards etc. should be made keeping child's safety in mind.

A simple dog or cat bite can cause rabies which may prove life-threatening after 6 to 12 months. Therefore, it is safer to give full course of anti-rabies vaccine to the child.

Keys of your child's success is in your own hand

By and large it can be said that it is parents who can make their child either a successful or unsuccessful. Parent's own mindset, attitude, education, ability to adjust with others and their skills to educate their child are most crucial factors for the child's success or failure.

The possibilities of the child's success increase when the parents try to find out his hidden talents and provide him the ample opportunities to develop them.

The parents who teach positive attitude to their children and constantly encourage them, then such children are achieving the great success.

Parents who understand that their child is a unique creation of God and the Almighty has a unique plan for him, children of such parents find going smooth in today's competitive scenario.

The child can remain equally composed and cool in success or failures if the parents give more importance to the child's self-confidence and understanding than to outcome of his exam.

Parents should understand that their child will learn not from their advices but from their behavior, attitude, thoughts, language and manners. When the parents understand this crucial point, the child-rearing becomes smoother.

When parents take the money spent behind the child's education not as an expense but investment, they increase the possibility of their child's success.

Parents should understand that education is not a monopoly of the affluent but it is an opportunity that every person can seize. This understanding can help the child's development.

Children living in honest, simple and realistic families have more chances of success.

There are more chances of success for the child if he had to make a bit struggle for learning things, if he was given responsibilities and if he didn't found somebody or other to help him at every stage.

The children repeat their success, when they are given encouragement at right time and acknowledgement for their achievements.

If the child learns to observe the truths and facts of life closely and learns to accept them, he can move ahead even in difficult circumstances.

The child's genetic traits, his friends, school, teachers, circumstances, good and bad experiences play important role in making him successful or unsuccessful.

The parents of academically weak children develop a feeling that their child will become disappointed for the successful future of their child. They think that only the good results can make good life. When such parents raise their child with a negative mindset keeping their results in mind, they push the child towards failure.

Parents should understand that results account for a mere 25% for the success in life. But the importance of qualities like self-confidence, courage, endurance and calmness is 100%.

Inside of timidity

Children in company of their mothers feel more secure and safe. Thus, they don't want their mothers leave them even for a moment. Child feels uneasy if you go out, perhaps to hospital or elsewhere, without informing him. Nothing can solace him in such situation. Thus, it is important to persuade him to accept circumstance before getting separated from him. Sometimes you can even use toys as an instance in order to explain things to him.

- Often mothers in order to frighten the child use name of demons, ghost etc. This creates deep-rooted fears in the mind and heart of child and adversely affects his subconscious mind.
- When the child is trying his hand on new things, the parents often discourage him with negative suggestions like – "Don't do this", "You won't be able to do it", or "It's not your cup of tea" – Such negative statements or the competitive atmosphere caused by parents between two children makes the child timid, negative, depressed, introvert and unsuccessful.
- Attitude of helping the child in every small matters, a narrow-mindedness that the child will spoil himself if he plays with other children of the society, ignoring the child's friends, trying to keep the child's toys strictly under your

charge – all theses affect negatively in day-to-day life of the child.

- Always trying to protect the child, daunting him with imaginary fears that he might fall down and hurt himself, not allowing him to go out, not letting him go out on a picnic and training camp, not allowing him to take part in sports – such approach of parents make the child timid.
- Often parents pressure the child to get good marks in exams. The performance pressure and the expectations of parents scare the child greatly even before appearing in the test. Rather than acquainting the child with where he may make mistakes, the incompetent parents load him with the pressure of results. They don't know that often the child learns great many things from failures. Therefore, such treatment destroys the child's self-respect, self-confidence, patience and ability to withstand the failures.

Parents must understand this.

- Children are the gift of nature. You cannot return them to nature in exchange of other ones. There is ***'No Exchange Offer'*** in it. You must accept them as they are and it is beneficial to change yourself a little than to attempt to change them.

Children understand the language of love, not of anger.

- You can control the child immediately by expressing anger, but on a long this proves an easy route to problems.
- Children love to learn through software, called – stories.
- Children learn majority of important attitudes of life by the time he reaches age ten. You can quickly inculcate values, good habits or teach him to set priorities and goals in life through stories and fictitious characters.

Your child is a product of your environment. The child does not taking birth as good or bad. The problems you face pertaining to your child are in fact caused by you only through your own attitudes and surroundings you created.

Children speaking lie, victim of tests.

Children learn to lie blatantly because of the fear of poor result, parents' expectations, the parents stand after the result and their inability to accept the truth. Telling lies relieve them from the tension of poor result. Parents love to hear good, but, not truth. Parents' such attitudes compel children to speak lies. Children often speak lies to their parents anticipating wrath and negative expression from them, if they (children) speak-out truth.

The learning patterns of the child

It is really essential for every parents to know that "How does their child learn?" For one single incident or occasion, each child can be reacting differently. The children grown up in the same atmosphere can show different reactions for likings and disliking. Similarly, all the children are learning in the same atmosphere. It is necessary to understand the different learning patterns and procedures. That is why, it is being said that, "If you are teaching to the child and he doesn't understand, then it is not his fault. You need to teach him the way he understands it.

A man took his sick pet dog to a veterinary doctor for the treatment. The doctor gave him a dose of liquid medication. After returning to home, he attempted to administer the liquid medical dose to his pet with every possible ways he could such as by spoon-feeding, forcing the pet to open his mouth, but, all failed and in the process he dropped the bottle on the floor and spilled the medication. Then the dog licked that medication. This is teaching us a lesson that we need to learn that every living being is accepting our teaching method or not.

(1) **The Children learning through Readings:**

Normally, in a class-room nearly 30-40 % children prefer to learn through reading. They have inclination towards reading. They are remembering what they read. They don't get tired by reading a lot. In fact, they are enjoying reading. While reading their mind is staying focused and concentrated.

(2) **The Children learning through Listening:**

Normally, in a class-room nearly 20 % children prefer to learn through listening and grasping through listening whatever the teacher is speaking about. For them listening is a natural way to learn. For learning, they are attuned to their teacher's voice, tone, and accent, sweetness of language, speaking speed and his expressions and gestures. This kind of children prefers to read less.

(3) **The Children learning through Activities:**

Normally, in a class-room nearly 15% children prefer to learn through activities. This kind of children have inclination towards teaching methods that apply audio-video equipments, learning and experimental tools, activities and charts, graphs, maps, models and designs applied by the teacher. During learning this kind of children prefer to listen music or with walking around or along with sports and games rather than reading by sitting at one place.

(4) **The Children learning through self-system:**

Normally, in a class-room nearly 10% children are developing their own system for learning, like first to read and then jotting down important points to remember them, and to later discuss them with friends for quick learning. Teaching others to learn, taking help of someone in remembering, learn that things quickly which is giving praise, to learn quickly from the teacher who makes learning enjoyable and other similar learning system the children are developing.

The children have different inclinations for preference for reading-time, place, ambience, management, and environment and so on. In some of the cases the children suffering from disabilities are finding hard to learn. Normally, the children are developing weakness in grasping or learning prowess because of several reasons like if he has born pre-maturely, the mistakes committed by the doctors during the pregnancy time, due to lack of breast-feeding by the mothers, over doses of medications given to the children and/or mothers, deficiency in eye-sight or hearing, genetic weakness, social problems within the family or at home, quarrels between the parents, behavioural attitudes towards him, lacking in facilities made available to him, too much control or total freedom offered to him, because of friends or atmosphere in the class-room.

Successful Parents and Unsuccessful Parents

Successful Parents	Unsuccessful Parents
Successful parents give importance to the child's qualities and overall character.	Unsuccessful parents give importance merely to the child's success.
They unveil the inner strengths and abilities of the child.	They enforce child to learn qualities which they feel look good on surface.
They support and stand with the child in the hour of failure.	They take hard stance and critical attitude when their child fails.
They always keep confidence and faith in their child.	They keep doubting their child's abilities and are overcautious in the matters related to their child.
They keep being the friends and companions of their child.	They expect performance from the child and act like the opponent of him.
They bring changes in themselves and try to get adjusted with the child.	They expect their child to change to get adjusted with them.
They create an atmosphere that suits the child.	They force their child to adjust in the atmosphere which is already created by them.
They see their child a reason to keep their expectations alive.	They see their child as an instrument to fulfill their expectations.

They attune their mind with the interests and inclinations of the child.	They want the child to attune his mind with their interests and inclinations.
They take the child's development as an end and the wealth as a means.	They take the child as a means and the wealth as an end.
For them, being parents mean making disciplined efforts.	For them, being parents is a burdensome responsibility and having pleasures is their final goal.
They can turn even an unsuccessful child into a successful one with patience.	They, out of their impatience, turn even a successful child into an unsuccessful one.

You can improve the child with inexhaustible patience

Usually the first child in the family is found more shy, introvert and dependable on others, even in small matters. This is true as he is being raised with much pampering and given much more facilities. He also becomes a subject of many experiments.

The child is always elder than his parents, in a sense that the parents become parents only after the child takes birth. More often, birth of the first child makes the parents more mature. Therefore, they rear the second child differently. So, usually you find the second child more active and smart.

When there are two children in the house, parents tend to compare them. This creates a sense of competition between the two children. In such an atmosphere the child who is weaker in studies finds himself a sufferer and becomes inactive.

Children become passive when not given chance to put their point, express their displeasure, freeness to discuss their problems, disappointments and feelings of injustice. They suppress their anger and often this anger takes a fatal form.

By being passive, children in fact start controlling parents indirectly. Eventually, the parents succumb to the child's inactiveness and stop him persuading.

Children, in a way, try to show their helpless state to the parents. This lessens the parents' expectations from the child, which in turn, reduces the pressure on child.

If the parents don't seat with the child and pay heed to his problems, if they don't allow him to express his disagreement and don't discuss things with him as and when necessary, they make the child passive.

Parents get good results if they act with a little patience, appreciate the child till he improves, act strict only when it is necessary and try to solve his problems.

Give a time limit to the child and stick with it. Make him to understand what would be the result, if this or that thing is not done. When you notice a little improvement, appreciate him immediately and results would get better the next time.

Usually, parents are the first ones who stop supporting the failing child. In case of the weak children, this is indicated by the parents' absence in the school meetings.

The day the parents would develop a supportive attitude towards their own failing child, the child would start giving best efforts for the success.

If the parents have inexhaustible patience, constant positive efforts and an understanding about the child's limitations and his inabilities, then to improve and make him successful becomes an easier task.

The Child is Speaking Unclearly

Mostly, the tongue is not causing the child to speak unclearly; however, normally the parents believe that their child is not able to speak clearly because of the problem with his tongue.

The reasons for unclear pronunciations:

- Because of his hearing-deficiency often the child is not able to hear the language properly, thus, as a result he takes longer time in finding clarity in his pronunciations. Just being deaf many dumb children are not able to learn the language and the parents are not able to understand this problem.
- If the formation of the teeth is not appropriate then also the child could speak few letters unclearly such as "t, th, k, and dh," and words formatted with usage of these letters.
- Many times stammering children stammered while speaking due to lack of confidence or out of fear. A noted Gujarati singer was stammering even while speaking a single statement, however, he was able to sing clearly without any problem.
- The child's genes are not responsible for his sweet-stammering and/or stammering.

- Even the slow physical growth and speedy learning of the language can also cause stammering into the child.
- The organs involved in the pronunciations and lacking in controlling of sensitivity of the mind also causing stammering in the child.

What help the parents can offer?

- Not to stop the children while are speaking, not to scold, and others should not instruct to improve their language.
- Accept the pronunciations of the child. Not to ask him to speak slowly or again.
- Not to train him to speak particular words or pronunciations.
- To give him sufficient time to speak.
- Tell the child about things that are boosting his confidence, to give him opportunity to speak, ask him to read aloud.
- Take away tension from him, encourage him and be patience.

Generally, if the parents pay attention to child, he can overcome from the suffering of stammering by the age of 10.

Even the adult persons also stammered in the situations such when they are much tensed, angered, in fearful circumstances, in and after nightmares, failing in the task, failing in performing the responsibility, in interview or in the presence of particular persons.

The Oscar Award winner movie "The Kings Speech" is a wonderful and very sensitive English film. The movie throws light on the life of the children suffering from stammering and depicting the roles of parents and teachers. The movie is based on true life story of Queen of English and her Father.

The children suffering from the stammering are able to sing clearly or murmur along the song while listening to it. If the fear of stammering is kept in abeyance from the mind of the victim then such children are able to speak clearly.

The Roots of Rebellion Attitude

There are the definite reasons for children's peculiar behaviour and its change, and often parents think that the child should understand their point or subject. But at the same time, the child is also having similar expectation from the parents that they too should understand their mind-set.

Whenever a child disobeys or refutes the parents' and/or elders' instructions, orders, advices, warnings and so on then he has some specific reasons for that...

- When a child is repeatedly given the same instructions then he ignores them.
- When the parents are labelling the child with insulting words like naughty, dull, stupid, idiot, useless, and outlined and so on then he resists to follow their instructions and advices.
- If the parents give instructions or advices to the child without heeding him or without understanding him properly or without bringing him into right atmosphere then he is not accepting them.
- When the children start to believe that they are grown-up and mature enough then they begin to give deaf-ears to the parent advices and instructions.

- Often the children test the levels of the parents to understand them by ignoring their advices and instructions and later they continue this attitude in future too!
- If there is hypocrisy or pretentiousness, insensitivity, unacceptability of emotions, rudeness and autocracy in the behaviours of the parents than the children don't accept or ignore the instructions and suggestions from them.
- Often, the children are avoiding giving answer in the classroom because they feel that if once the answer is correct then the teacher will always ask them to get-up for the reply. Because of the similar psychology, the children are adopting similar attitude at home with thinking that if once they are conceding instructions from the parents then they will have to always follow them!
- If the parents don't understand the psychology of the children and think that they must heed their instructions then it causes more problems.
- If the children are kept under strict control, repeatedly given negative instructions, freedom is taken-away or their friends are not accepted than also they avoid their parents.
- Taking their opinions for the decision pertaining to them, giving importance to them, their point is accepted one way or another, their self-respect is guarded, giving them a feeling that they are being trusted then the children are following the instruction and advices from the parents.
- The kids are your children, not property. In your behaviour if the children feel that you are acting

like you are very powerful man and your decisions must be accepted by them then to establish their own power the children starts to oppose you.

- If the parents don't give quality-time and don't spend privilege-time with kids then they avoid mother and father.
- Often the child attempt to convey a message by avoiding the parents, he is not able to make them understand and parents not able to understand thus to make them realise he opposes them. However, if the parents accept his resistance and ask him with patience for the reason of his resistance then they will come to know it.
- When the parents are just giving 30 minutes daily to the child. And of that they are spending 12 minutes in interrogating him, 5 minutes in finding out his mistakes, 5 minutes in correcting him, 3 minutes in giving their opinion and just 2-3 minutes to let him talk, then, the child is listening them with the deaf-ears.
- Whenever you have oppose to the child then move away from him, get pacify, give him space and time to express his resistance and if an attempt is made after sometime to make him understand then the child is giving very good response.
- When a tired father returns home from the work in the evening and then if mother immediately complaints about the child, under the circumstances the father gives negative and harsh reactions. As a result, when father arrives home the child feels his problem has arrived

home, not a solution. Therefore, when the father arrives at home then the child attempts to runaway, hide, pretend to be engrossed in the study. Thus, when the attempts are made to make talks in such uncomfortable atmosphere then the children avoid listening.

Brhamakumari Shivaniben has rightly said, "The father gets tired by the evening after whole day work in the office, so he returns home with completely discharged battery. And in the morning goes to office with a fully charged battery and generally when father meets the child then normally he would be out of energy. Thus, how could he spend a quality-time with the children?"

The problem could be solved easily if the parents are changing themselves slightly rather than trying to change the child completely.

The Time Management for Child's Success

The **TIME-MANAGEMENT** doesn't mean time-table for study or activity. The Time-Management also doesn't mean to keep the child running with the clock, but, necessary to develop a sense to understand it.

- **The Time-Management** means to manage quality-time for the child from the total time available by you.
- **The Time-Management** means management of in perception of the age of child, what should he be shown, which places he should be taken, and what reading he should be offered.
- **The Time-Management** means to develop maturity of adaptation of child's changing emotions, sensitivities, demands, requirements, facilities, freedom and trust with his changing age.
- **The Time-Management** means to plan-out the opportunities for the child in the extra-time he is having besides the study-time.
- **The Time-Management** means to make a balance of time that due to study the child is not deprived of his childhood, life doesn't become a burdensome, not engulfed in the competitions, and happiness and liveliness don't vanish from his innocent eyes!!

- **The Time-Management** means the child passes his childhood in happiness yet he learns everything essential.
- **The Time-Management** doesn't mean to memorise the questions and answers of the lesson on Gandhiji but to manage to visit his famous Sabarmati Ashram to peacefully make deliberation on the values of virtues in the life of Gandhiji.
- **The Time-Management** means an art to make relativity with the speed of the time-clock.
- **The Time-Management** means a perfect formula consisting of speed, power and accumulation for the growth.
- **The Time-Management** means to develop a skill into the child so that he can match himself to keep pace with time and tide.
- **The Time-Management** means the child himself performs the task and the parents help him into understanding it. The management to prepare the child for forthcoming situations, challenges, questions, to understand the problems, all these means the time-management.
- To set up a calendar, a pencil and a day-planner on the study-table or into the study-room of the child so that he can learn to make planning for the coming days.
- A table-clock should be placed on his study table and to make him understand that how to finish the home quickly so he can spare time for sports and Television.

- The parents should set a well planned time-table for self and should discuss in a manner that the child understands it and show that how punctual they are about their time-table, and then the child quickly learns **The Time-Management**.
- **The Time-Management** means how to divide the works into small modules, to teach the child how to bifurcate the preparations for the exams. For an instance, when only 30-days are left for the exams then whether to make a perfect plan for him running up to the day before the exams or just to give him advices and instructions and leaving rest on him.
- To maintain a time-diary to make him to realise that in which activities how much time he has wasted.
- Include him in the planning and preparation for activities like tours, cleanliness, kitchen, arrangements and so on.
- As he develops his habit and skill to wake up on alarm time, to get ready neatly and timely, becoming punctual about time, and so on then he should be appreciated for these and be rewarded with something.
- **The Time-Management** means to teach the child how to save time, how to shorten or speed-up the task, what preparations should be done before the time of task, how to think ahead of time, not to lose against time, not to see the time in frame of period, days, months or years but in the purview living and life.

The parents should develop a habit in the child to use the internet for learning time-management through Online Time Management Game and other similar information.

I am vividly remembering an unforgettable incident about the Time-Management. During an interview for the post of a principal for our school, one candidate had arrived late for 45 minutes without any proper reason and kept the members of management waiting. Though all the members were in favour of his selection for the post, yet, in simple and clear words I said, "How could we appoint the man for the post of The Principal who has no value for 45 minutes?" The Principal had lost an opportunity of the job with a monthly salary of almost Rs. 80,000/-.

The students lately filling forms for the competitive exams, candidates arriving late in the exams, the employee arriving late in discharging their duties, the leaders coming late at venue to deliver the public speech and organisers starting the programs later than scheduled-time are the victims of the **Poor-Management.** Even if these people are strong, the circumstances and success do not give support to them for long.

Why do children become inactive

In order to understand the behaviour of children, their habits, interests, tastes and their likings, one really needs to know the child psychology and thus understanding their social and mental development.

Sometimes kids, who are very active, in a gradual manner reduce themselves into a state of inactiveness or almost turn passive. And, following this they tend to become rude and even develop an ignorance trait. Generally these kind of behavioural traits are seen more among the first child of the family. In many cases, children who are constantly being egged on or counseled by their parents slowly develop a sense of passiveness. Especially among the first child of family who is the centre of all the care and receiving complete attention and help at each step of their early lives by their mothers; be it eating meals, carrying out chores for getting ready for the school, dropping him for school bus and again receiving him post-school time, makes him completely inactive.

Other aspects that contribute to first child's gradual inactiveness and passiveness are: - when sibling rivalry takes place among two kids of a family or while living in a joint family, when performances of two kids are constantly being compared, when another child's capability is praised again and again, and at a time when a child is criticized in presence of another kid.

Sometimes insistent parents' constant attempt to control their wards by imposing over-disciplined routine leads to a situation where either the kid becomes passive or makes him aggressive, and starts ignoring the suggestions, instruction and directions given. Also expresses their protest, anger and many times while doing so it may resort to acts which destroys things around.

On occasions like when kids are not able to express their own struggle, disappointments or their dependency; or even for that matter while unable to solve difficulties renders a feeling of being unsafe which makes passive and aggressive. Moreover, issues which lead them to passiveness include when their needs are not met, their hobbies and interests are ignored or not paid any attention. Following this child almost stops oral communication and starts ignoring parents, and grows up hardhearted feelings.

Many times passive kids make things done as per their will and indirectly start controlling their parents. By non-cooperative attitude force parents to agree to what they say and also creates negative trend by flimsy protests.

A Child can be made active if parents try to understand and remain careful in their behaviour for all the above mentioned situations. Situations could be improved if parents stop forcing kids to change, instead, try to bring changes in them. Changes could be brought into kids if proper steps are taken after understandings the reasons for change in them. Those parents rushing to clinical psychologist for very normal behavioural issues of their wards actually need to contemplate bettering their behaviour and atmosphere around. One got to be a childlike with their children. And, one needs to understand kid's mistakes and failures from theirs age perspective.

The Breeding of the good habits

Almighty confers the children into the parent's hands like a clean slate. And, it is the overall conduct of the parents, their behaviour, their ideals – all these creates conducive surrounding for the child to learn and pick up. Normally children adopt and adapt to all good habits and culture after a prolonged observation of their parents. And, thus it is aptly said - parents must keep in mind that children learn more by not hearing but by observing.

In order to encourage development of a gifted personality of their wards, parents must pay close attention to the following things when it comes to their own social attitude, attire, attitude, manners, courtesy and politeness.

Always address children with utmost regard and maintain their respect and dignity. Teach them the importance of three words; 'Please', 'Excuse me', and 'Thank you' from the early days of their childhood. While infusing these, parents must teach two words; 'Sorry' and 'I will not repeat' to their wards and best way to do it is they themselves put into practice of using these words constantly.

Learn to take wards' help in daily household chores and never miss an opportunity to appreciate them whenever they take part in it. By doing this you will encourage a sense of responsibility in them and thus making children to realise its importance and feeling of being helpful to others will make their personality more beautiful.

Treat their friends in a good way. Teach them how to deal with their friends. Try to inculcate a sense of sharing in children; where they are fine with sharing their toys and other stuff with friends. Don't make children possessive.

It's always advisable to address children using their names. Have conversation with them in a clear language. Also develop a habit among them so they place things at proper place in the house and first implement things at your end that you expect to see in them and practiced by them.

Remain alert to inculcate good habits among them; like washing of hands before taking meal, following table manners while eating, eating habits, diet and doing physical exercise regularly.

In order to develop politeness in children; customs, consideration and commonsense plays a very crucial role in their upbringing. If you find any faults in their behavior, it becomes imperative to focus on three things; appreciate their little achievements, create a proper place to showcase their trophies, certificates and prizes they have won, and express word of commendation for their abilities. To change their habits deal with them utmost patience.

Allow him to take his own decision. Seek their opinion while choosing clothes or any other things of their liking, and always offer them options instead of directing them to do what you had in mind. Leave that place immediately for some time and ignore it if you find kid's behaviour intolerable.

If you feel that the present surrounding may lead to bad habits in your children then try to leave that place or make an effort to give them best environment. Don't always give in to children's demands. Don't do everything as per their wishes. But stop them at right way whenever they are wrong and prevent them from becoming stubborn. In order to change their behaviour do not encourage a habit among them of receiving a gift or a prize for that, do not make efforts to bring conditional change in them. Make sure you don't miss a chance to appreciate child's maiden effort of improving their behaviour once you instructed them to do so. Also keep in mind that fighting or punishing children never helps in bringing change in their behaviour.

To become parents is an incident but to live up that parenthood forever is nothing short of disciplined and dedicated actions to accomplishing that. Raising children is not duty but a festival to be celebrated life-long. Childhood is a golden period of life. Do not let it become burden. Children do not improve by just giving them facilities, physical comforts and conveniences. Remember this – putting children into hostels, making them leave home or keeping at somebody else's place is a solution of your issues and not kids'.

Try to use this positively that children could learn good or bad things by considering a role model either from TV characters, from stories or even somebody ideal in the family.

Over-discipline insisting parents

Generally parents, who insist discipline and good behaviour among their kids, do resort to instructions, advises, punitive measures, physical or mental punishments and for that matter emotional punishments too. Such recourse done by parents often leads to creating many problems with children.

Most of the time parents take this type of punitive measure to bring instant changes in their children. However, results of such futile actions are often short-lived. Parents tend to give physical punishment to their wards because they lack proper understanding of how to improve kids' behaviour in a short period.

Usually parents, who suffer from a mentality of wielding total control over kids and being a sole proprietor, often resort to physical punishment to their wards. Those children, who have grown up in such punitive environments, do deal with their kids in a similar fashion when they become parents. Such measures create many issues in child's psyche.

- Children who were continuously meted out with physical punishment suffer from inferiority complex and eventually lose self pride, and become emotionless.

- Punishment develops the feeling of vengeance and protests among children
- Because of punishment children become emotionless towards their parents, start ignoring them and many times behave in discourteous manner.
- Children accustomed to such punitive measure develop an attitude of negativity, abhorrence, disgustful, anger and destructive mindset. They behave like that.
- Parents, who insist a gag order on their kids in their presence, wants their kids to act as per their wishes and do what they say, often creates lot of problems in the upbringing of the kids.
- Those parents, that lose patience and resort to punishing their kids while trying to make them learn things and improve, break the emotional bridge with their wards. And, thus kids develop a habit of running away in presence of their fathers. And even try to hide them or finds like-minded friends.
- For kids, fathers who are habitual of treating their wards with harsh words and punishments, often become a problem instead being a solution. And apparently ruin the life of kids having a delusion of being stern disciplinarian.
- In real sense, parents must develop actual understanding of parenting. They must comprehend the difference between teaching, preaching and punishing and for that they must keep in mind the following things....

- Need for punishment will not arise if children are patiently given an understanding of what is right and wrong in their behaviour instead of punishing.
- Kids will commit lesser mistakes if they are given a clear understanding of difference between a process and the result.
- An improvement could be brought about if children are clearly instructed about the results of their behaviour arising in future and not just being indicated of something to them.
- Stern disciplinarian parents must remain careful about their speech, actions, behaviour and self discipline, and become role model for their wards.
- Kids need to be heard patiently, must satisfy their curiosity and ought to be given opportunity to showcase their abilities.
- For creating a beautiful family, we all and children need to improve. Sometimes a belief like 'We are true and perfect' creates trouble in the raising of a kid.
- Children require support during failures, guidance when commit mistake, encouragement while competing, need self-confidence when up against a danger and always looks for your support and backing.
- God shapes every child differently and their lives are not just meant to compete. It is needed to find and encourage skills and abilities of theirs which is unique from other kids.

Successful parents could even transform failed kids into a bright success while failed parents may make their bright wards a failure. Successful parents will take side of answers while those failed will resort to doubts and questions. We need to ask ourselves that where do we stand?

Behaviour change – A mega battle

When it comes to bringing an expected behaviour among their wards, every family has a different definition, environment, system, training and approach. However, majority of parents waste their efforts, time and power by becoming curer rather than becoming preventer. If you insist certain disciplinarian actions from your wards then it becomes imperative to know that kids learn 50% of the things from home-environs, 25% from school and own attitude and approaches while rest 25% contributed by relatives, neighbors, friends and pre-natal values. Behaviour is an outcome of a definite reason.

Children resorting to mischievous and annoyingly playful behaviour in presence of guests are deprived of freedom at home. This mean these kids live in a very controlled environ and experience the freedom only when some guest arrives.

The main reason behind infants, toddlers or even kids taking to crying and in turn attract somebody's attention is for to demonstrate that they are also an important individual out there. Sometimes even a complaint for toilet is also meant to bring the same thing to your notice.

Mindset of those kids, that lies, hide something or even do not share entire details related to their school life, are conditioned that way because of fear, punishment, threat or consequences of past response from their parents. And, the feeling of getting punished if they tell the truth often inspires them to behave in such manner. Those parents who are unable to digest failure of their wards inspires the latter to lie and do not reveal entire information.

Parents, who hold a constant negativism, taunt, finding faults and not accepting their wards' friends, either fail in their own performances or have lacking in themselves. Kids, bombarded with words like 'you will never learn', 'you will never be able to do it', 'am certain you will fail', 'you are a fool', 'you are irresponsible', do hang back in competitions.

Many times children, who living in such environs and made to compete with their cousins constantly, makes them failure in their efforts and gradually develops a feeling of hatred towards home. And many times such children expresses deeply rooted anger towards their brothers and sisters.

Parents need to get matured, instead of kids. Children learn and pick up things from closely surrounded environs. Inculcating good habits, education, politeness, civility and conduct among children calls for genuine efforts accompanied by extreme care. In order to improve it, it is important to reach the causes of visible weaknesses among your kids. Children do not improve or change by mere instructions and punishments.

It is imperative to make them realize the consequences of bad attitude. Few of the examples need to be understood generally to bring changes in the children.

- *It is to be noted that a failed student, who once received great accolades and words of appreciation from his teachers after playing a humorous character in a school play, became one of the most acknowledged humorist of Gujarati literature. Today people know him as – Mr. Ratilal Borisagar.*

A child will never look back and keep on improving even if a little improvement or change in him is being accepted and appreciated by their parents. Parents, who live with certain restraints, fight with realities of life, lead spiritual and self-disciplinarian life and remains constantly alert to develop good habits among kids, do achieve success in most of the parts of bringing up of children.

For parents, chances are less of succeeding in extending an ideal upbringing if they try to change their wards offering facilities, physical comforts, and money or even for that matter resorting to negative attitudes.

Things like - helping children, have proper understanding of importance of physical comforts, reading of good stories, a quality time spent together, parent's patience in understanding their problems, efforts made to know the correct information, natural ability to change habits and consciousness of parenting helps bringing the desired result among your wards.

Positive reaction and praise

The most positive reaction, feedback and appreciation or praise from the parents to their wards always makes the latter emotionally stronger. Generally parents who shows anger or contempt towards their wards' mistakes, failures or even shortcomings often lacks the habit of appreciating positive attitude in their kids. Because of this the kid is deprived of much needed inspiration for developing a positive attitude. One must not miss an opportunity to praise and appreciate children when she or he very positively carries out common activities. Children deserve compliments when they put their things in place, school bag at its proper place and keep their shoes properly.

When should you praise the kid?

- When child does well in any of the work
- When there is any improvement in their work
- Shows Positivity about learning new things

Parents must use effective appreciation rather a simple general act of praising, such as parent must use 'I like you when you do the work like this and I am proud of you'; instead, 'You did this work very well'. Other effective ways to praise include; saying 'you are a promising child', give a pat on their back, give a hug, kiss them, lift them, give them big round of applause, a signal of thumbs up and caress their head.

Clarify The Positive Attitudes:

If your child washes his/her hands before sitting for a meal then make sure you always illustrate this behaviour before others and recognize it, and appreciate in a language that it comprehends. Make a point to tell your kids that 'You follow the instructions very nicely' without fail. This inspires kids to practice good attitude more repeatedly and leads them to follow and implement your instructions.

Clarify The Reasons:

Children will not repeat the mistakes and will welcome the positive instructions if results of their behaviour and attitude are clarified to them and made understood. For example, if a child assists in arranging the house just before arrival of some guests, places things in order or does this entire job on his/her own then it certainly brings a sense of relief and pride for parents. The parents must tell their children that his/her presence makes them much comfortable and also make your wards realize this feeling.

A child will become more responsible, wise, and mature, and starts developing a positive mental attitude when the relation between reasons and results becomes clear to him/her. For instance, teach the kids to accept any notes made by the class teacher during teaching session for their mistakes and this will make kids become responsible, so they could avoid such notes in future, and pay attention to it. Children will definitely change his/her attitude if parents help them in understanding the mistake committed during the classroom and guide them on how to avoid such situations.

However, children takes to complicated, hardened, negative and irresponsible attitude when parents fails to accept the mistakes of their wards committed in the class, taunts, defends their wards and, in fact, especially when try to blame it on the teacher. The same child afterwards starts ignoring or rejecting parent's instructions, advice, becomes inattentive, rude and subsequently the problem keeps increasing.

The parents, looking for a positive change or improvement in their wards, must not ask them to do anything by promising any reward or cash or even a gift, in advance. But they should only be rewarded just to encourage for such repeated improved behavior, only after if parents are able to notice some real improvement in his/her attitude.

How to increase child's reading habit?

Our entire education system is exam-oriented and based on memorizing the texted knowledge. Securing good marks has become the only objective of our education system. And, as a result of this system the 'individual development' of a child has suffered an unimaginable loss. Because of such education system, we have got large number of good businessmen, but, could produce very few visionary industry entrepreneurs. It has produced good office workers, but failed in offering new and innovative research to youths, who could take on their aims with much more passion. 'Reading' is one such an important factor that shapes an individual and therefore it remains to be encouraged and developed among kids.

For children, in order to imbibe a good reading habit, at very early age of standard 3rd or 4th, bring them books made for their age group.

- The books that you give them has to be colorful & illustrative, having texts in big size and convenient to use.
- For kids aged around 5 to 7, avail them the books such as short stories, anecdotes, fictional stories, or stories related to Panchtantra or

King-Queen, mountains, jungle, animals and birds or magazines like Champak.

In the beginning the parents must sit together and read out stories of their kid's liking. A child could certainly become good reader and a book lover if this habit is continued till the age of 5 to 12. Or try to show them picture in the book and let them speak and weave a story around it, inspire them to speak and prompt to ask questions, and slowly the child will start reading the book regularly.

Allow them to buy books, create a collection and give a place to create their own library. Parents need to sit with their wards and listen to the stories that they read, and/or discuss it. Schools should organize book reading, reading skills, story writing competition, dictation, story games and staging of theatrical comedy of small kids for all those studying between standard 5th and 7th. For celebrating occasions like birthdays, the schools should motivate the kids to either buy or even gift books to their friends.

Children can develop great interest in reading, if families disallow them to watch TV and stories could remain only option of entertainment for them. One must take their wards to book exhibitions, libraries and encourage them to have good collection of books. Also try to arrange one good small library in the house.

Moreover, schools could arrange to have book reading competitions and also consider giving marks for book reading.

A child who has developed a reading habit from an early age will eventually become a voracious reader at a later stage of life.

Benefits of Reading:

- Even amidst stressful moments a child could relax while reading.
- Reading habit brings education related maturity in a child.
- It develops child's ability to think, know and understand for reasoning.
- Also it makes a child creative as reading inculcates good thoughts, ideal life style and power of imagination in them.
- It keeps the children away from Television.
- Those kids watching TV witnesses almost 10,000 crime scenes comprising of loot, thefts, fights, rapes and cruelty till he/she reach the age of 14 and eventually it affect their mindset and psychology.
- Constant encouragement by parents for reading, efforts by the schools, and reading habit of a student, makes the task of shaping up of a 'talented personality' an easy one.
- It makes children's speech more effective as reading improves their word-power and sentence formation.
- It is undisputable that a good speaker has always been a good reader.
- It brings out a child's feelings, thoughts and attitude towards faith or belief in the matter of

morality, religion, society, family, nature and humanity.

- Reading only makes a normal human into a good human being, good writer, poet, creator, film script writer, director, journalist, actor, teacher, leader, thinker, saint, a story-teller, a person who gives a religious discourse or even an essayist.
- Today reading has become an inevitable need. Gujarat Government's and Chief Minister Narendrabhai Modi's "Vanche Gujarat", is a praiseworthy mission which needs to be stretched to each and every classroom of the schools.

If a parent wants to do some real good work at very early age for shaping their ward's life in the best possible manner then they shall encourage him/her to develop reading habit.

How to keep kids busy?

What all a kid could be asked to pursue during free-time?

- Children keep themselves busy in reading if they are made to develop reading habit at an early age of 5 - 6 years.
- They could remain occupied in a good way if they are kept engaged into activities such as sports, drawing, music, dancing and craft skills from the age of 7 years.
- Tasks like house cleaning, arrangements, decoration, decency, assisting in cooking, sprucing up of house, purchase and making them learn how to take care of things can also keep them occupied.
- Also aspects that could keep them engaged positively include; how to make good friends, how to keep relationships, how to get mixed with friends and carry out works and if they are made to learn how to share their things with friends in order to use it.
- Parents need to see that computers and TV should not become free-time friends of their wards.
- Ask them to develop interest in swimming, horse riding and cycling.

- During vacation time, start sending your wards having age of 12-years or more to nature camps, environment and adventure trips in company of a matured coach only after checking safety standards.
- If your wards have special interest in history, geography, science, mathematics or literature and so on, then find out such development centre for respective subject areas and involve them into it.
- Children who are into collecting stamps, coins, cards, leaves, feathers, information collection for birds also remain active and busy.
- They could also be kept busy by parents by taking a daily walk with them, taking a stroll in the garden, and/or playing a game of chess at home. And, the best parents would be those who are also having reading habit thus they can keep their wards busy by telling stories and encouraging them to read too!
- Send them regularly to nearby skills development centre, community science centre, mathematics or language centre and help in developing this habit for long term.
- Once kids are involved in such activities, parents must drop any of their fear or doubts, and try to find out on how their wards could transform this habit into a lifelong fulfillment.
- Parents must remain alert and make enough efforts for such activities.

- Alert parents could use this free time creatively and innovatively to help their wards come out of their weaknesses.
- Take handwriting improvement for an example. Encouraging your wards for this will be an ideal use of time.
- They could be put into the Centre for Languages, Speech Improvement, Personality Development and other such courses with an aim to improve and enhance their manners and attitudes.
- Make them to learn Yoga, its different postures and Pranayam.
- Personally, I have constantly felt that the youths and kids' centers run by different religious sects are really doing good work. This is not an option of development but certainly becomes useful in instilling values, civility, interests, humanity in them.

In today's community, no special facilities for the children are considered in our professions, schools and even government's urban planning. There is even scarcity of good playgrounds, equipments, coaches and encouraging environment.

I saw a public school in Huntington in New York's Long Island, which charges no fees from the students. The school is spread over a 250 acre of campus area. And, after watching the Olympic level running tracks, a library that could make any Indian university feel ashamed and the level of coaching at the school, I realized that India has miles to go in achieving similar progress.

Discord among parents is unbearable

A child's existence, development, his/her health and self-confidence completely rests on the normal relationship shared between parents. Easy, tolerant, gentle–pleasing, good and cordial relationship between father and mother can always have a very positive influence on the children. While circumstance where the parents experiencing disagreements, arguments, difference of opinion, disputes or divorce are going to have negative effects on the psyche of a kid.

For a principal, who is struggling to develop an association with a child, the struggle and strife experienced by a divorced couple brings the utmost sad affair in the entire process of education. Though the separated parents might be able to get the custody of a child but they utterly fail to restrict negative attitude despite giving their wards best of the facilities and physical comforts. Even after a year of divorce, gradually children's attitude tends to become negative, harsh, dejected, angry and protesting one. Also such children's result too gradually gets lower. Children of such separated parents later on grow a sense of insecurity, lack of self-confidence, indecision and nurse negativity in subconscious mind while moving on in their lives. Many times such children take to the negative activities and crimes.

For kids, it is the relations with parents that are more important than that of getting physical comforts and facilities. For them conversation is more significant than the instructions. It is the gentleness which gets preference over advices. Kids, who do not even learn after thousands of instruction to be helpful to others, may well pick up it in just mere one instance mere while observing his/her parent's dedication towards each other; mother and the father.

The tradition of giving away oneself for the other selflessly, being tolerant to each other is breaking away as an individual has been drifting from values of joint family to nuclear one and from having an individual room to more secluded privacy including separate TV sets and range of facilities at their disposal for each family members of the home under one roof. Therefore sometimes family bonding and values are stronger in the people living in smaller houses.

Divorces affect the boys the most. In such cases, boys seem to face more problems while girls turn out to be more tolerant and able to put up with its consequences. Also the feeling of insecurity is seen more among those whose parents shifts the accommodations and schools more often.

Divorce tears apart the individuality of a kid into two. The struggle of getting custody of a child literally reduces them into a property that the mother and/or father hell-bent on acquiring. For kids these types of struggle among parents stoke a feeling of hatred towards both.

One day a divorcee mother came to meet her son, a third standard student Nikunj, who stays with his father, who already had submitted a court letter of having child's custody with him in the school. In wake of this, the desperate mother took a firm stand, seeking one glance of her son even through window-glass of the classroom, but denied permission to see her son one-on-one. Even the mother was apprised about her son's pitiable plight in such a situation and persuaded to settle the issues with her husband. And, when Nikunj was called inside the school office his moist eyes were speaking everything, especially the happy moment of seeing his parents together. Without wasting a moment, the trio was requested to watch the movie – *Baghban*.

In tenure spanning over 20 years as a principal I have aided so many such settlements between husband and wife; and even witnessed changes which the couples accepted wholeheartedly.

A husband and wife should always discuss their problems only in the absence of their children. Couples must not treat the child differently with an intention to influence in such a way that the child surrenders to one of the individual, either mother or father. Do not expect solutions of your issues from your children. Parents must show immense respect for each other and if possible, address your kids with honour. Show extreme tolerance over small-petty issues and refrain from getting into argument or quarrel.

Instead of trying to change the other person; one should bring a small little change in himself. One should develop a strong sense of ***'let bygones be bygones'*** and try to forget issues. Beware of the fact that attitude, talks and issues of some other must not disturb the peace of your house. Avoid discussing or dragging the family members and common relatives of either husband or wife into the conversation. Letting the past goby, one must focus on bright future. Family is only pillar of our human-life system. All the struggles of life, development and happiness will turn into pain and unhappiness if family matters get bitter and marred by allegations.

Children say 'No' to school

- Children at the beginning of their school life, either going to nursery or attending junior kindergarten, make protest against sending them to schools because of sheer insecurity felt by them. Children fear that once they are left alone at the school and mother gone away as they will never see her again. The feeling of separation from parents and/or members of the family makes the kid to protest against going to school and even cries, and resort to all sorts of protests within his/her reach.
- While students from 2nd to 12th standard protest against joining a new school because they do not like to leave their present school environment.
- In the early days of schoolings, children do protest against going to school if his/her feelings have got hurt by any of the teacher or student; or issues which he/she has encountered, any comments about conduct, language, appearance or even behavior.
- Many times comments made relating to religion, sect, race, caste, name, father or mother gives a feeling of hatred to the child toward school. Thus, he avoids going to school.
- Even factors like poor academic results, poor show in some performances, failure or even for

that matter performance below expectation levels could also become one of the reasons for a child to protest and not go to school.

- Other reason that could make a child to protest against going to school in the beginning not able to make friends in a new school or even for that matter his/her dislike towards the teachers and the system he/she is just introduced to.
- Even a kid's emotional bonding towards a close relative or grandparents visiting the household may emerge a reason for his/her dislike to go to school.
- In one such instance, a third standard student, Daksh Raval suddenly started protesting against going to school, teachers and attending classes. This boy started threatening to run away, leaving school and even kill himself. But it was later on it was realized that the reason for his all erratic behavior was his grandmother living in a village, who was visiting them and Daksh was not willing to leave her. In fact he wanted to stay with her only.

The parents must check the above mentioned reasons whenever a child protests against going to school. A child needs to be assured of security to make him/her determination of going to school stronger and need to be prepared mentally in order to get mixed with the surrounding easily.

Schools need to give their teachers a special training to make the newly admitted students feel more comfortable and receive acceptance in the classes.

Following a complaint of class teacher, Aanush, an 11th standard student, was called in principal's office for talking to girls only in the class. When asked about, it, Aanush replied to me, "Sir, as yet have not become friends with who are boys in this school. Those two girls I am talking to are decent. I know my limits. Teacher made comment about this in the class is hurting me. Sir, you tell me, what is my fault?"

We need to understand, learn and change to behave with the new generation. We need to change the "spectacles". Tomorrow it may happen that a class teacher may not wish but boys and girls will be sitting together. This is not a challenge of tomorrow, it is a destination.

Pillars of relations

During a training workshop for principals of the Ahmedabad City, then Education Commissioner Smt. Jayanti Ravi had asked the participants to write an essay on "I Remember My Teacher". And, majority of the principals had written several pages describing instances of remembering those primary teachers who had left lasting impression on their minds from their schooling days. After this, all participants were asked to raise their left hand holding papers and put right hand on heart and asked to the self that will they be a part of such essays 30 years from now when students whom they taught will be told to write such an essay?

Teacher is not just an instrument giving information. It is not essential that the teachers should be highly proficient, but, surely be having a good knowledge on the subject. What is more requiring is good nature, inexhaustible patience, and virtues like soft, tolerant, gentle and pleasing, emotions, modest and polite, kind, courteous and friendly attitude, so that his personality could be friendly and likeable among the students, teachers and parents alike.

A teacher has to have a marginal quality of motherhood along with weightiness of father. Teacher is expected to have an understanding of reaching to the last student of class. Teacher got to have an ability to move on taking along every student with him and a skill to motivate that develops a vision of tomorrow and self-confidence in children.

A successful teacher is one whose entry into the classroom is eagerly awaited by the students, if he fails to reach on time. Victorious teacher is the one who is living in the heart, mind, and home environment of students. A successful teacher is a role model; whose feet are touched by students even after a span of 25 years.

The one who knows and feels the pain of students and strives to endow them with abilities bringing novelties in his ways is a good teacher. A successful teacher is one who has always been awake, adopting new approaches, and offers new things to students.

I want to recall one incident that I witnessed in an ordinary primary school at Detroj village where I saw a truly living principal. I saw an academic instrument shop which was being run by students and I was amazed to see them practicing something unimaginable. They picked up whatever they needed and put the money in a box. No checks or person to monitor it. That time I realized that it is better to put the box of honesty before students than giving lessons of honesty using a book. In same school I also saw unique laboratory teaching student draw map on sand squares using scale of cord. Not necessary that you will find a good teacher only in big school of a city. Even I have seen good number of real teachers, who is having a real zeal for teaching with heart in small primary school in villages.

It feels like a politician has entered into class under the garbs of a teacher when he punishes students, shows partiality, utters foul word and talks of hollow ideals.

The warm relationship between students and teachers is making the school's atmosphere lively and humanly, and leaving long lasting memoirs of true relations. It is also visible in the training of principal. It is also visible in the success of school management's vision and can be felt in the society that values its teacher with a strong sense of pride. It is also visible in the system rewarding teacher's abilities. Truly showcased in village's ideals and is surely experienced in management system that backs the teachers who are doing well. It sparkles in the eyes of students and visible in the wings of proud parents. It shines equally in the reputation of family. It is also felt in the remains of the last rites of the teacher as well.

Successful Teacher and Unsuccessful Teacher

Successful Teacher	Unsuccessful Teacher
A successful teacher touches heart and inner-being of his students.	An unsuccessful teacher feeds only information in child's brain.
A successful teacher transforms the information into knowledge, and then teaches it to the student.	An unsuccessful teacher converts knowledge into information.
He thinks of all-round development of the children.	He just thinks about marks-oriented improvement in students' results.
He makes learning process a joyful experience.	He mechanically follows teaching process.
He turns knowledge into science by referring book as a resource.	He considers books as everything for teaching and turns knowledge into information.
He converts education into knowledge and brings success to the students.	He converts learning into a competition and baffle students into the webs of mark base system.
He gives priority to encourage weak students.	He focuses only on bright students.
Students find solutions of their difficulties in him.	Students see him only as a problem, not as a solution provider.

Students keep faith on their teacher and give a special niche in their hearts.	Students see him just a paid-teacher and then forget him.
Every moment students have spent with their teacher becomes a pleasant and memorable experience for them.	Every moment students spend with the teacher passes mainly as a stressful and disgustful experience.
He is like a divine-man and is the oxygen to the school.	He is an unsuccessful man behind the shadow of a teacher and is a destroyer who creates problems.
Students keep trust on him and can go ahead in their education.	In a puzzled educational system, a student does not feel comfortable.
He has a vision of 'How to shape-up the students to be a part in nation building.'	He is busy with in fulfilling his own interests through teaching.

Successful Principal Vs Unsuccessful Principal

Successful Principal	Unsuccessful Principal
A successful principal creates student friendly atmosphere.	An unsuccessful principal prepares kind of students who adopts prevailing atmosphere.
A successful principal recognizes the potentials in the student and provides them opportunities to grow.	An unsuccessful principal force the students to adjust themselves in available opportunities.
He instills 'A Vision' into the teachers; generate 'Interest' among the students and provides 'Solution' to the school.	He creates 'Division' among the teachers, 'Constrain' the students and 'Pollute' the school.
He implants school's potentiality on to the student sitting on the bench.	He uses students' talents for hefting treasury of the school.
He, who gives directions to the teachers and gives warmth to the students, can become a successful principal.	In him the teachers see a directionless leader and the students feel an unlikeable captain of the ship, is an unsuccessful principal.
He who feels pain of the class-room (students) and has very strong sensibility to become a successful principal.	He knows the pain of the chair (position of principal) but his sensitiveness has become null, so he is an unsuccessful principal.

The one who focuses on student's difficulties and problems rather than propagating good results of the school, can become a successful principal.	The one, who gives more importance to the propagating the results and turns his head away from the frustration of students, is an unsuccessful principal.
A person who guides students and their parents can become a successful principal.	A person who keeps distances from meeting the students and parents is an unsuccessful principal.
A person who transforms efforts of the students, teachers and school into a success can become a successful principal.	A person who after sitting on a peak of fames, ignores the development of the school is an unsuccessful principal.
A one who discharge his duty first as a teacher, then as a father, and lastly as a principal can become a successful principal.	After becoming a principal, who seizes to be a knowledge imparter and a fatherly figure of the school, is an unsuccessful principal.

A Vision is Essential for Career

Our entire educational system is working with keeping an eye on percentage based results. Majority of the parents are deciding the career-line for their wards on the basis of percentage they have obtained in the Std. 10th and 11th. The entire system acts like the child's academic excellence has no connection or links with his/her interest, talents, inclination, skills and career. Right from the kindergarten level the parents are evaluating the performance of their children's on the percentage they have obtained rather than looking at their natural abilities and talents.

Rather than bringing out the talent and personality of a child, today our entire education system is moulding him into a robotic machine that just stores and rote the information and pouring them out in examination-hall; and mostly a machine that runs after the money.

The Government, System, Society, Media – altogether have sowed only the seeds of competition, jealousy, impatience, and show-off and as a result the trend of mass scaled corruption, attraction for money and wealth have rampantly grown-up in the society.

Our Divyapath School (Memnagar division) had organized a 'Career Carnival' in the year 2008-09. In the Carnival, the students had prepared over 250 projects as per their interests and inclinations: each project was showcasing present days' career opportunities and next generation career for the future times. While, kindergarten children had played a skit depicting the essential language-skill, smartness and alertness requiring for becoming "***The Airhostess.***" During the event, over 30,000 people, mostly parents, had visited the school and after that I noticed that the focus of the parents have shifted from '***Results***' to '***Career***'.

Ahmedabad city's well known Chartered Accountant had made two unsuccessful attempts in the 12th Science, before he opted for the ***Commerce Faculty*** and became the Chartered Accountant. His failures were the results of overlook of one important fact, when he was in 10th Standard, he had obtained very good 58 marks in Arithmetic, but, his performance was not good in the Algebra. If his parents had noticed this important fact at the time of results of his 10th standard, I am confident that then they could have easily saved three important years of his academic career and prevented him from suffering of 'depression, frustration, and failure' for that span of time.

Who is sowing the seeds in the brain of our children that the success of life lies only in becoming Doctor or Engineer? Why our children are just dreaming of 'to become a Doctor or an Engineer only?' Why our children are not showing passion for the fields like Music, Painting, and Sports? Why our Children are not searching for a career in the field of 'Wildlife Photography'? Why result of our research is always ending in 'Zero'? Despite of having such a vast coastal line, why are we backward in the fields like swimming and marines? Why only a handicapped person from Japan and a blind man from Scotland are thinking to climb the Mount Everest? Why Gujarati youths are running away from joining Army, Navy and Air Force?

An answer to all these questions is lying in our education system which we have set up as a career for them (children).

Today's our success is the success of the percentage obtained on a good memory. Now-a-days, all our ventures are aimed at generating capital wealth. All our growths are visible in possession of materialistic valuables, thus ultimately, rather than living in a good life style, we are living in a world that is indulged in a competition in possessing materials and means.

For our kids, we are securing good percentages in the exams, but, we are not able to teach them, how to survive in the times of failure? Today's youth are able to ride the motor-bike at very high speed, but rarely knows, "What is a time-management?" He knows how to use a high-end mobile, yet, doesn't know that the Mobile is for a 'Management Mobility or Entertainment Mobility?' We are not yet able to bring in an educational syllabus that teaches 'A respectable life can be lived with a bicycle, rather than with a high-brand car only.' Our mind-set of 'talking of high morale but doing a lot of wrongs' has not yet changed.

Let's come on, teach our children an art of living rather than pursuing them into the competition of percentage; and to realize that the prosperity of the family is not lying in money and means, but, in eating and sharing together. Money ultimately delivers nothing but tension, bad-habits, poverty and diseases; therefore, we must teach our children to live a healthy, happy and simple life, rather than converting them into the money-earning robots.

Teacher's Despair at the Triangle of Development

Standing at the triangle of 'Education, Society and Success', "I am envisaging a different picture than what the world is watching; and every teachers should try to visualize the same picture just like me and the system should give a proper training to understand it.

Sameer, who was a bright student and throughout securing the 1st rank and winning respect of everyone in school, while, another student of his class, Amit, who was mostly getting promoted, this was the picture of class-room of 1980s which is entirely different today. Now, Amit is the most successful man in the society; he is a contractor; very wealthy with having all amenities like cars, luxurious home and others. Contrary to this, Sameer is an ordinary engineer and living a very ordinary life of a common-man. So, the scenario has completely changed now!

Once, a student, who was honoured as the best student for his decent attitudes and well-mannered behaviours and proven very bright in study too, is now a doctor and practicing with very low moral to cheat the patients and having no norms or ideals. And Maulik, who was always receiving insults for his weaknesses during the school days; is now with his noble works has become a real social servant and a donor in the society.

In school-years, one who had won the state level prizes for his essay on 'Maa' (Mother) and his copy of the essay was distributed among all students; today, he is not willing to take care of his own mother, while the eldest son of the same mother who didn't know how to write an essay, is proven to be her best son with taking care of her like son 'Shravana' of Ramayana! Similarly, yesterday who was the naughtiest student of the class and expelled from the school, is now a very successful businessman and the one who was winning laurels for being the good student has become a high-rank corrupt government officer to become an undesirable element of the society.

I vividly remember, whom the school was selecting as the 'Best Monitor' and honoring for his 'Leadership Ability', is today doing an ordinary job and one who was never elected to lead his class in the school, is now a successful MLA.

I am not able to understand that the student who had all facilities and the best teachers at his disposal, arranged by his wealthy father, was unsuccessful academically. While another student who was hailing from a hand-to-mouth family, is now a successful engineer.

The teachers need to ponder over this reality that the successful results in the school examinations are neither guarantying of 'A Successful Life!' nor giving a confidence to fight against small problems those being poised by the life. Every year, now, 5-7 engineering or medical students are ending their life due their inability to handle stress and/or depression, but, this suicidal tendency is hardly visible in the students of the art-faculty!

Every year, It is happening that many of the students, who have had secured higher percentage of the marks in the school examinations, are often hanging themselves by the rope just before or after the results at higher-level of education, while failed students are continuing their journey of life happily and cheerfully to leave behind their ***'Failure'** to achieve success in the life, later!* I have constantly observed!

Even after having experience of 25 years in the educational field, I couldn't understand one thing that the children who were appearing very ordinary, dull, colourless in the school life. After a gap of 20 years, they have had groomed oneself as a very healthy, strong and full of confidence young man. In contrast to this, healthy, bright and good-looking students have developed oneself as a very ordinary looking youngster, after 20 years! This reality is depicted by noted writer Shudha Murati in her book 'Man ni Vaat' (A tale of an inner-mind), which should be read by every teacher.

It surprises me that the government is providing training to every school, yet, only 40% schools are having very sparse success ratio, while the private coaching classes, which have not been given any proper training, are having success ratio of 95%. And the teachers of these private coaching classes are being considered as the '*Successful Teachers*' in the society!

I am really puzzled that the teachers whom the government had selected and appointed on their merits, their presence in the class-rooms are not being wished at all by the students, while one who had cleared his 12th exams with many difficulties and passed out from B. Sc. in the pass-class is the most successful teacher today! The government and the System is not willing to accept the fact that the higher percentage has no connection with the success of teaching; and this fact is really a despair for me being a principal of a good school!

I feel, ***'a total contrasting scenario between the class-rooms of yester years and the present-day society!!'*** A father, who is a successful Kathakar (religious discourser) and preaching to bring social reforms or guarding traditional values of the society for a betterment of the civilization, has a son who is always indulging into frolicking and addicted to several heinous bad habits.

Similarly, one who is known as the Business Guru and charging very high fees to attend his lectures on 'the Business Management,' has failed in his own house-management and family and his family-life is on total mess. So his night and day life is completely contradictory to each other and giving a totally opposite scenario.

Among today's most politicians and preachers who are delivering lecture on high moral and ethos, citing the examples of Mahatma Gandhi and Swami Vivekananda, are the highest corrupt people in the practical life. We know this open secrete, yet, these corrupt are allowed to speak freely and at will, while the real practitioners of 'High Thinking and Simple Living' hardly get chance to express his thoughts in the public life. Thus, in reality 'Our society is the world's biggest Hippocratic Society!'

I feel like laughing when the parents are paying respects to the schools securing higher ranks in the Board Exams. Media is also honoring the bright students. Whenever I see these, a thought is crossing over to my mind that why we are not thinking to honor the students placed in remote villages or tribal and interior areas or in bordering zones.

Not a reporter, but, a teacher is the **First-Person** who is closely witnessing the transformation in the society. Not any leader, but, the teacher is the **First-Person** to realize and experience the transformation. Not any social-worker, but it is the teacher who is clearly visualizing that which way the country is heading for! But, I think, the teacher is not sensing that he has a core-competence to form 'A Successful Society' or he might not be interested in knowing this fact!

All trainings are incomplete as long as the triangle of 'Vision, Path and Situation' is not properly grasped.

The mechanism, which the System is attempting to make '*successful*', is giving a very depressive inner-scenario and it is difficult to say that the training programs based on the planning are capable to set it right!

The Investment made on teachers' training is the best investment. But, lacking of good learned educationists and failure to express the pain of the class-room, and modules prepared with some good-words for the out-dated curriculum of B. Ed, will not be able to help much. Therefore, the schools of Vibrant Gujarat will need a revolutionized training to make them vibrant-schools in the real sense!

A Restless Mother for Hand-Writing Improvement

A 4th standard, girl-student, along with a class-monitor, entered into my office with her lesson-diary for not doing her homework. We had a rule, if any student having more than 10 complaints in his/her lesson-diary for 'home-work not done' then matter should be reported to the Principal.

First, I sent back the accompanied monitor to the class-room, then I softly asked her, "Dear, why are you not doing your homework?"

She responded with saying, "Sir, I am doing my homework regularly, but, my mother is tearing them away from the note-book as my hand-writing is very poor."

"And sometimes, my mother is beating me too!" the girl further explained and then she exposed the beating-marks on her legs!

Then, I summoned her mother to my chamber and held a detail deliberation with her in very cordial atmosphere. Later, I conveyed a meeting with the parents who were unhappy about the bad hand-writings of their children. For all those students, I chalked out a 'Hand-Writing Improvement' project and appointed a lady-teacher, specifically for this!

The results were wonderful! The project proved very successful for all of our schools. Even few teachers had also taken benefits from this project!

A lady teacher, Ms Bhavini Suthar, who had been handling this 'Hand-Writing Improvement' project, earned good fame and name from its success in the Ahmedabad city. Ms Suthar now earns Rs 20,000-25,000 per month from her this skill. She has also published a book about this.

If a proper attention is given to the incidents happening into the school, they could bring a massive change into the life of students and teachers.

A small effort had brought happiness to many families. Turned a teacher into a writer! And it benefited to all.

It is the job of the Principal to break the ice of 'Time-Table' and 'Circulars' and to sense the pain of class-room ***(students!),*** if this is done then the good results will automatically follow rather than forcefully dragging them in to the class-room.

At the Root of Science Stream

The school authority took a serious note of the prevalent trend in 12th standard students, when only 20 out of 120 students opted for the Science Stream. This bitter reality was taken by us as a serious challenge and as a result we implemented few concrete remedial measures:

- A weekly-visit to the Science Lab was made compulsory for the students from 7th – 9th standards.
- A series of science based tours, exhibitions and programmes were conducted on regular basis in the school.
- A series of the lectures by the learned personalities from renowned institutions like ISRO & CSC were planned out at regular intervals.
- Presentations and exhibitions showcasing the career opportunities in the Science stream were also done at frequent time gaps in the school.
- 'Science Quiz and Debate Competitions' were organized among the students to generate their interests for the Science stream.
- Science-Math carnivals were done at the regular intervals in the school.
- The lectures from the former Science students who have made a successful career and life were also conducted in the school.

- Counseling of the bright students, who are not opting for Science stream just because of psychological fear, were also done.
- The Group Projects to generate interest for Science among the students were organized; and each of these groups was being headed by a teacher, who was assigned a responsibility is to finish the project successfully.
- **The Science Teaching Aids Competitions** were arranged for the class 9th students of the school.
- ***'Robotic Make'*** inter-school competition was organized which attracted participation from over 85 students of 24 other schools of the city.
- **'Career Awareness Programmes'** had been organized for over 800 students of the 9th class to elaborate the benefits for opting for Science stream.

As a result of these measures, in the next academic year 70 pupils of total 120 students of the class 9th had opted for the Science stream If this result can be attained by the sincere efforts of a one-school teacher, then with united efforts of all the schools what cannot be achieved!

Dawn Begins With Prayer-Peace Mantra

One lady professor from the University had attended our school's ***Training Programme*** and she delivered a beautiful lecture on the subject: ***'A Teacher must touch the heart of the students!'***

During the ***Training Programme***, she had narrated her own a true life experience.

During her lecture in the class of S.Y.B.A., one of the students was constantly looking out of the window with his eyes set on the sky. This simply annoyed and made her very angry, so, she instructed him to leave the class and see her in the office during the recess-time.

Later, when the student entered into the staff-room to meet her, he disclosed that he is a son of farmer-father and hailing from an interior village of the Sabarkantha district. And, then he handed over a post-card, written by his father, to the lady professor.

On the post-card, the father had written, "Dear Son, I don't have money to pay your fees. Nobody is lending me money even on interests as weather condition is like drought prone, however, if the rain starts, then anyhow I will arrange to borrow some money for you. Anyway, if your college authority doesn't permit you to attend the class 'due to non-payment of fees', please come home for few days!"

"That is why I was looking at the sky with a hope that if the clouds could appear in the sky, then I will not have to leave my study at a half-way and return to home. I am taking food only once in a day to save some money and having just one pair of clothes to wear", he stated his condition almost with an emotionally choking voice.

The disclosure of this bitter reality, which is almost similar for the most Indian farmers and having the same fates, had touched my heart and softened me as my anger towards him had gradually evaporated with a thought crossing over to mind that "How much the fate of Indian farmers is depending on the 'Good Monsoon' season!"

However, often such hard struggling circumstances are toughening the child to groom into a strong man. Therefore, I believe that for grooming a person into 'a man with a strong character' adverse circumstances like lack of money and food, deprived of amenities, and others are sometimes proving to be ***'A BLESSING IN DISGUISE'!***

Even the gold must pass through the fire to take a shape of jewellery!

We make a collective morning- prayer at 7:00 O'clock in the school precinct with an idea to interlink and converge the 50 individual mornings of each student to make it as a single morning and finally to link it with the morning of the teacher. That is why, it is called 'Prayer, Peace-Mantra!'

The Training Changes the Person's Perception

A change in ***the Perception*** to looking at the problem, often finds a solution within the problem! The change in perception, finds an answer within the question. Change in the perception is changing the situation itself!

A man's perception can be changed with a proper training. Therefore, the Training should be such as that it changes one's ***Perception.***

When I was governing the D. P High-School, in the year-2000 I had attended a lecture on ***'MAKE YOURSELF A LEADER'*** delivered by a well-known speaker on the subject as a training programme at a handsome fees of Rs 25,000.

That Leadership Training Programme had entirely changed my perception on ***'Governing an Institution'***. As a result of newly found perception, I decentralized the entire administration. Most of my responsibilities were relegated to the teachers of the high-school division.

The teachers had geared up themselves to take-on the new role of 'An Administrative Officer'. In turns, every teacher was given an opportunity to administrate 'Prayer and Stage Management.'

Thus, today my high-school section has not just '8' teachers but all of them are like '8' Principals as they all have a capacity to administrate the school ***"SUCCESSFULLY."***

As now I am less burdened, I have focused my entire energy in further expansion of my institution. As a result of change in my perception, the growth path of my teachers and institution has completely been changed.

After attending the training programmme ***'MAKE YOURSELF A LEADER',*** it completely changed my entire perception for ***The Training.***

I think, now first we need to the change perception of every institution for: ***The Training.***

The private corporate-houses that have set-up a new benchmark for High Quality Administration for their employees, are now conducting Management Training Programmes for the government officials too at the regular intervals.

Today's teachers' mind-set are as such 'To continue teach with the same methodology', 'Circumstances are adverse to implement any change in my teaching style or method', 'What is my interest or gain?', 'Is government going to confer me with any award?', 'Am I going to have any monetary benefits (mainly salary-rise)?' 'My fix income of the salary is secured.' All these need to be changed as these mind-sets have simply killed our instinct of 'competition', 'adoption of a new approach and novice ideas'. Therefore, any institution that has done a little change in its method and has gained better performance with it; is drawing an attention of everyone and thus making a giant stride in its progress.

This wave of change is taking place at the schools where the principal is having open mind-set. The changes are possible only at the schools where teachers have not lost their faith in the system.

A new perception that 'The training is firstly going to benefit the individual teacher too, not just the institution' should be developed.

If 'A' is given 1 mark and 26 to 'Z' than the total of ***'ATTITUDE'*** will be 100-marks. That should be examined, understood, accepted and implemented.

A Challenge: Adulthood Training to Teenagers

- The occurrence of genetic and biological changes in the body due to adolescence age amongst the teenagers are often bring changes in their behaviours, that often give a false impression of indiscipline and unknowingly invite punishment for that.
- The natural attraction towards opposite-sex due to adolescence age amongst the teenagers, often resulting into behavioural changes thus creating an atmosphere of 'indiscipline' in the class-room.
- The psychological influence of movies, television and other medias like internet, channels, CDs, DVDs, etc. on the teenagers ultimately create an atmosphere of 'indiscipline' in the class-room.
- The psychological changes caused due to adolescence age are often resulting into an atmosphere of 'indiscipline' in the class-room.
- The happening of physical, behavioural and mannerism changes among the teenagers due to adolescence age are often causing problems in maintaining the discipline in the class-room.
- The psychological influence of family environment, society, and religious identity on the mind-set of the teenagers and their adverse impact on the class-room atmosphere.

- Lack of training to teachers on psychology of the teenagers, the methods of punish adopted by the teachers for the teenagers and remedial measures taken to prevent physical punishments.
- The transformation period from childhood to adolescence age among the students, particularly in the girl-students, naturally brings large-scale behavioural changes due to changes in their body-hormones. The girls are becoming more aware and conscious about their clothes, hair-style, appearance and body-look. Moreover, sometimes they become less-attentive in the class-room study. When these things come to the notice of the teachers, they often make comments; sometimes even very sharp verbal comments or punitive actions. The girls are mostly not capable to discuss their womanhood problems openly with the teacher. They try to share these problems with only their girl-friends. As a result often the teacher is experiencing an atmosphere of indiscipline in the class-room.
- The teenagers mostly preferred to make jokes, fun, comments etc. within the same aged groups of friends. The boys are becoming aware of their physical growth and often try to exhibit their physical power to prove that they are more strong compared to others. Their nature is becoming more enterprising, aggressive and risk-taking, which are often being reflected or witnessed in the class-room. It becomes more visible in behaving with the neighbouring friends or class-mates. Often they are found indulging

into making fun, jokes and small mischief in the class-room. The teachers have to be very cautious, restrained and refrained in dealing with them (teenagers).

- In the Teenage-years, it is natural amongst the boys and girls to get physically attracted towards each other. Particularly, students of Std. 8, 9, and 10 are acting with each other like they are the open competitors or rivals to each other. In the class-room, they make accusation on each other about their respective mistakes, attitudes and behaviours. Sometime they even get indulged in the verbal duels or exhibit aggressive attitudes or behaviours towards each other. All these are very natural happening because of their reformation age span. Therefore, the teacher should handle them with care and caution with the adoption of the practical solutions. However, without understanding the mind-set of teenagers few teachers are getting up-set and taking panelizing steps!
- During the adolescence-years, body changes are occurring visibly fast among the teenaged students. The rise in sensations and growth of genial organs are becoming very lively and their growths are becoming easily visible on the body. The students are becoming more aware about their body. However, as they are not having the complete knowledge of adulthood, it is quite obvious that they are becoming inquisitive and curious! As a result, they mostly discuss about it among their groups of friends. Sometime these

discussions are entering inside the four-walls of the class-room. In the modern times, the students are not able to restrain themselves from effects, particularly bad-effects, of sexual-knowledge presented through today's mass communication gadgets and facilities like mobile, internet, CDs, DVDs, photos etc., sometimes such information even penetrate into the class-room. Bringing of such materials by one student in the class-room, generates curiosity among other students and causing problem of discipline. Some teachers are not ready to accept these as a natural course or trend among the teenage students, therefore such teachers consider those students as the wrong-doers and take disciplinary steps against them.

- The Films, Television and other mediums like Computers, Channels, Internet, Newspapers, and Adult-Magazines are making very deep impact on the soft and adolescent minds of the teenagers. These mediums are affecting even the dress-code and styles of the teenagers. At this age, the teens are often seen expressing their heart's feelings and sexual attraction for the opposite-sex through love-letters, cards, sehr-sayari (love poems) etc. Few teachers consider these behaviours as ill-doings and take disciplinary steps!
- During the adolescent-period the girls and boy are becoming very sensitive about any personal comment, particularly downbeat one, in the presence of each other and such statements

sometime make them depressive. Because of volatility of adolescence, the teenagers are quickly and easily grasping the negative things/habits. Owing to adolescence-problems sometimes they develop or assume bad habits. Disappointment in the contest during the adolescent-period often produce feelings of hatred, rebellion, despair and the feelings to take revenge and to establish that 'I am competent of doing so!' For e.g.: the students weak in learning frequently enter not on time in the class-room, making mischief, passing comments. He does all these to prove that he is capable of everything, which, in fact, is his mind-set. His, this attitude often causing situation of unruliness in the class-room.

- During the adolescence-age, the body of teenage boys and girls are forming more muscles and stronger bony structure. Thus, they develop more interest in activities like out-door games, picnics, songs-music, dance and others. Sometimes boys and girls who are under more influence of the western civilization can't prevent themselves from expressing their feelings through western customs like singing songs, playing music or making facial and bodily gestures. Even occurring of such incidents unknowingly (as a reaction of subconscious mind) in the class-room or within the school is often annoying some teachers who rather handling them tactfully than go for disciplinary punishment. Such sharp and harsh reaction from the teacher is erroneous, in fact, it is better to show more tolerance and soft approach.

- In the teenage years, family circumstances are also playing a vital role in behaviour and mannerism of a teenager. The teenagers get more easily affected by different partitions of the society like Rich-Wealthy, Middle and Poor classes; a modern satellite family or traditional united family; different castes, tribes, religions. The frictions among all these divisions become in fact evident during their individual or groups talks, arguments, accusation, and competition and so on. As an outcome, they often make disorder in the atmosphere of the class-room.

Important is Teaching or Testing?

When the ancient **Guru Dronacharya** took the test of **Kauravas and Pandavas,** it was a test of their **'CONCENTRATION'**. And only **Arjun** had passed it! When **Upagupt, a great Buddhist Monk of 3rd century B.C.,** took the test of The Great King **'Ashoka',** then it was a test of his **'CONSISTENCY'**. And to pass this test, the King Ashoka had to give-up everything of his! Similarly, when Swami Ramkrishna Paramhansa took the test of Narendra to become **Swami Vivekananda**, then he had to abandon his home. The pages of history are filled with hundreds of such various instances of the tests conducted by the Guru for his disciples or students.

Today's our 'Examination System' is a half-century old. In this system, 'we are just testing memory-power of a student and sensing happiness in conferring a certification of the percentage on that base. And therefore, **the test has become more important than teaching**.

Can't it be possible to have a Testing System that is freeing a child from any written test? Can't it be possible to have a Testing System that does not fearing a child? Is it not possible to have a Testing System that scales the **qualities** of a child rather than his **memory-power**?

To logically understand the difference between TEACHING and TESTING, we must compare them:

TEACHING	TESTING
The Education is a system to shape-up a child.	The Testing is a method to give satisfaction to the educationist.
The Education is a system that constantly keeps the child normal, active, and happy.	The Testing is a method that initiates a sense of fear, tension and pain in the child.
The Education is a system that turns the class-room into the Heaven.	The Testing is a method that turns the class-room into the Hell.
The Education is a medium that constantly drives a child further towards growth.	The Test is an obstacle set on the path of development of the student.
The Education is a system that teaches the art of living to a human. And teaching him to find out an answer to the problem.	The Test is breaking the confidence of a man and converting him into a 'Contest - Machine.'

This doesn't mean that there should not be an examination or test; and also not mean that the examination is a problem. But, surely it is a problem that demands an immediate pondering, if the children are ending their lives by hanging to a rope just because of the fear of exams or their results. The examination system requires changes. The exams should be teaching 'LIFE MANAGEMENT' to the children. They should mostly generate sense of satisfaction among the children.

Once, the birds, animals and wild-animals had decided to set-up an examination system in the jungle to decide 'Who is the superior among them?' The Lion said, the test should be only for the roaring. The Monkey said, the test should be for the jumping only. Then, the snake said, the test should be of sliding only. The Fish said, everything else is useless, if you don't know the swimming. Therefore, they decided to conduct the different tests for each animal according to their natural skill and talent, gifted by the God! Thus, after the tests each animal secured first-rank in their respective fields of the ability. At the conclusion, the fox questioned that "If we, animals are having such common sense to understand this simple thing. Then, why doesn't the human understand it?

The existence of exams-fear among the children, in fact, is more of fear of the parents and friends. They (children) have fear of their teachers too. This ratio of fear has diminished among the children from the day since we have announced that 'not to pronounce students' results in the class-room and not to write the ranks: First, Second and Third on the board.'

Psychology of the Teachers Making Physical Punishment

1. When a teacher loses his patience to understand the child, then he is giving a physical punishment.
2. When a teacher is not possessing sufficient knowledge to teach, then he opts for a physical punishment.
3. When a teacher drags his personal problems and questions into the class-room, then he attempts to release his anger and frustration of that on the innocent children.
4. When a teacher faces confrontation with the school management and/or parents, then he attempts to raise his arm to punish the children.
5. When a teacher fails to understand the reason that makes a child naughty in the class-room, then he opts for a punishment.
6. When a child goes against the expectations of the teacher, then he gives a punishment.
7. Frustration, depression, lack of enthusiasm or work-load can also generate anger in the teacher that often ultimately makes him to punish the students.
8. Not fulfillment of his desire or failure to conduct class-room as per his will, this often leads to raising of his arm to beat the children.

9. To prove that he is stronger and more capable than the child, he raises his arms for beating.
10. Just like in cricket, a wicket-keeper makes an appeal to divert the umpire's mind from noticing the wide-ball, similarly the teacher attempts to hide his weaknesses by diverting the minds of children by punishing them.
11. When a teacher is lacking of capacity to make the children to understand his teaching, then he attempts to conceal his failure by punishing them.
12. The teacher's lacking of command over the proper words and language for teaching or in personality, and then he attempts to raise his personality by giving bodily punishments to the children.
13. The teacher suffering from the psyche that, "Whatever I say is always truth." is often trying to suppress the class-room. As a result of this any reaction from the children lead to a punishment from him.
14. The physically and mentally weak teachers are more prone to deliver a punishment to the children.
15. The teacher having lack of control on self is having tendency to punish the students.
16. The teacher suffering from prejudice, feeling of revenge and confrontation are more prone to give punishment to the children.
17. The teachers having weaker eco-socio background often take shelter from their frustration by punishing the students.

The Curative Steps to Curtail Physical Punishment

- To give a training to the teachers about adolescence-age.
- To make teachers to understand the effect of adolescence-age on the body and mind of the teenagers.
- To make teachers aware about role-model of the teenagers.
- Training for positive governance of the class-room.
- Giving understanding of depth of disciplinary action.
- Impart them with the knowledge of applicable rules, penal codes, scope of imprisonment and fines and police actions for giving physical punishments to the students.
- A training to generate feelings of good governance in the class-room and to convert class-room into the Heaven!
- Coordination and training among the students through co-education.
- To conduct parental training.
- A healthy debate in the class-room on 'Punishment to Students'.
- To make the teacher 'SENSITIVE' about the problem of the students.

- To organize activities that enhances coordination and cooperation among the students.
- To coordinate the activities of group-activity, value based and ethical education.
- To organize activities that is based on the life of great, renowned personalities of the society, state or/and national levels.
- To find out a positive and creative ways to de-addict the youths from bad habits such as chewing of Gutkha and tobacco. For instance: To organize the cancer-awareness tours to the Cancer Research Centre for the students, who are addicted to consuming Tobacco or Gutkha.
- Training to positive attitude.
- To bring the children's mind-set out of the barricades erected in the name of 'Religion, Sect, Cast and Economical' groups.
- To make attempts to create healthy atmosphere in and outside the school.
- To organize the creative programmes continuously.
- To organize good story telling, poem reading, movies and short plays at regular intervals.
- The school's daily prayer is made as a subtle, non-formal medium for teaching.
- The displaying of the newspaper cuttings, articles, photos that are criticizing teachers' punishment to students, in the teachers' staff-room.
- The screening of the movies that upheld the values of humanity in the school.

- To conduct competitive programmes in the school and to honour the winners at public functions to create sense of respect and honour amongst the students.
- To organize the lectures and talk-shows with the leaders and prominent personalities of various sects and religions to generate feelings of mercy and respect for each religion among the students.
- To readout 'The Inspirational incidents' in the prayer-meet or to display on notice board. To organize similar programmes in each class-room, from time-to-time, by the teacher.
- Formation of a Disciplinary Committee in each class-room.
- Organise various 'Disciplinary' camps, training programmes and activities.
- Organise NCC & Scout activities in the school.
- Organise tours to various camps and exhibition conducted by the Home Guards, BSF, and Army.
- Organise tours to the institution and organization known for their disciplines, punctuality and precisions.
- Organise mass scale social works such as cleanliness drive, plantation-week etc.
- Organise Psychology Training Programmes for the teachers in which lectures delivered on subjects like 'Child Psychology', 'Discipline', and 'Punishment'.
- Group discussions among teachers, parents and students on 'Discipline and its related problems and their solutions'

Memorable Experiences of the School

- The class-teacher of the Senior K G asked Mansi to draw a fruit-tree. Mansi drew a tree and on its branches she drew rectangle fruits with each having a straw inserted from the top. The surprised teacher asked, "Mansi, which fruit is this?" Mansi innocently responded with saying, "It is not a fruit-tree, but, it is Fruity, where the tastes of all the fruits are available."

  This funny incident proves that our education system is not imparting any reality knowledge and having weaknesses in its base. We need to learn a lesson from this incident. The teaching about the tree, fruits, vegetables and crops in the class-room should also have some practical sessions by visiting the farm or forest.

- When I noticed my nephew, a student of Junior K. G., was studying from his picturesque alphabet-book by looking a picture of truck with saying, "'Kh' for truck. 'Kh' for truck." I was shocked and surprised to learn that he didn't know that "Khtaro" was another name for the truck.

  When the definition of a word is changing, it simply confuses the child. Vanishing of a word from our language and usage is like a process of erosion of land. Similarly, words like "Ba-Bapuji" and "Maata-Pita" are gradually disappearing from our day-to-day language.

- Earlier in the last 10 minutes, all activities were coming to a halt and every student was just waiting, with his school-bag packed, for ringing of the last-bell to leave the school. The teachers were stopping teaching. With an idea to use this collective wastage of huge teaching-time for constructive teaching, we decided that every student will march from his class-room to the main-gate of the school with loudly speaking of THE NUMBER-TABLES. After six-months, we found the results of the Math's have shown a remarkable improvement and interest of the students have also changed towards Math's and every student had memorized THE NUMBER-TABLES by Heart!!

For the Success not the Person, but, Attitude should be Changed

Mr. Kaushik Mehta, a teacher joined our school as in his former school of the Ahmedabad city, he was a surplus teacher. Academically Mr. Mehta was a teacher of Mathematics but at heart he was a Music Guru. He was the well versed on key-board to create the music that could touch every heart that listen to him. He was the best key-board player of the city.

I decided to entrust Mr. Mehta with a responsibility only of teaching the music to the students. And in just one-year's span the school had shined out at the city level in the field of music amongst all the schools.

Mr. Mehta was writing the songs and then composing and sings them with full joy and emotions from his heart. This started making him living merrily in his Personal World! In just 4-years' span Mr. Mehta had bagged over 100 awards and trophies for the school and become the most favourite teacher of the entire school.

Mr. Mehta admitted that "In my former school, where I spent over 19-years as a Math teacher, I never got an opportunity to touch Harmonium, while at the D. P. School I had never been prevented from teaching the music along with the mathematics. The previous school has been closed-down now due to lack of students, while in D. P. School, we have to higher the security guards to control the mob of parents pushing-in to get admission for their wards in the school."

For The Success not The Persons, but, The Attitude should be Changed.

The Principal is the Provenance of Inspiration

During my long career as the teacher at the New Vidhya Vihar Girls School, the learned principal Ms Divyaprabha Mehta had asked me to prepare a script for a debate competition and she encouraged me a lot too!

Since then I started to read and write a lot. A bright student, Miss Rekha Chaudhary, once asked me and my principal to write a script on one subject. On the basis of those two scripts, Miss Rekha won a Gold Medal in the renowned S. R. Bhatt Debate Competition. The winning of this gold medal had instilled a great amount of passion and inspiration in her to keep on writing her thoughts and expressions and to deliver them at the various debate competitions.

Earlier Miss Rekha was very naughty student, but this one victory of winning the Gold Medal had completely changed her mind-set and the goal of the life.

With passing of the time, Miss Rekha become a very good orator and addressed many public meetings held during the political election of the local politicians. Later, even she herself fought an assembly election for the Gujarat Assembly and become an MLA. Today, in Gujarat Congress she is a prominent woman-activist and many a times she is narrating her experiences to me.

The teacher's job is to brush-up and lit-up the talents of the students. If that is done, then the flames of his/her talent get shined-out in the entire society.

Inspired once to write a script made me a writer and Rekha Chaudhary an orator. Thus, I salute Ms Divyaprabha Mehta for her ability to spot a right talent in every individual.

The Inner Sentiments of a Student

My name is ----------------------. I am studying in 12th Science stream.

Sir, I don't prefer to roam around uselessly with friends to waste the time. I am putting lots of efforts for studying well. However, my results are not very impressive. In the first test, I had got only 69%. So what should I do? How should I prepare myself to improve my results?

I want to do something different than most others. I want to fame my name at the world level. I also have a desire that my name being recognised along with other prominent and giant personalities of the world. To achieve these desired successes, what kind of efforts I need to make? What planning should I do?

I am constantly living under the fear. I am feeble. I am not interfering with anyone or anything and staying very silently but for the same good reasons others are giving more trouble to me! For instance, few days ago one of my class-mates had borrowed Rs 10/- from me. After few days, he had paid-back Rs 5. Recently, he told me in a threatening tone, "I will not pay back the rest of Rs 5. What can you do?!" Out of fear of physical harms, I could not do anything to him. It is not a question of small amount of Rs 5/-, but, the way he had duress me was proving that I am feeble and weak. This is making me frightened and depressed.

One question that constantly hammering my mind is that "If, the people will continue to harass me, then, how will I live?"

I am not able to speak or express my thoughts and ideas from the stage or even in front of a small group of four-persons. My legs start shivering and shaking, mouth is unable to deliver words, and tongue is getting stammered and mind is getting blank. I am not able to get easily accustom with others. Due to these inabilities, what sort of difficulties I will have to face in the life? Sir, what I need to do to overcome my weaknesses? To become strong, agile and leader, what should I do?

Sir, I am suffering from stones in my both kidneys. I am the only child of my parents. They have a lot of expectations from me. I love them a lot too. For my good academic career, my family is making all possible efforts and pushing aside all difficulties. I am very aware of all these. But, what will happen to them if I die due to any of these diseases? Whenever, I am seeing others happy and enjoying the life fully inside and outside the class-room, then, a question is engulfing my mind that why can't I be happy like them? Why none of them and me only is suffering from those diseases? Why the people are just troubling me only? What wrong have I done to anybody? All these things are troubling me a lot and putting me under constant pressure. I don't understand what to do?

Sir, you and only you are the one who could solve all of my troubles. You are the Guru for me. You are like ***The God*** for me and my ***The Ideal too***!

I have total faith and confidence in you that only you can pull me out of all these difficulties.

I request you to keep this as a confidential and secrete.

Thanks a lot!

I will never forget that Day!

One day a Himalayan spiritual guru and saint, Vishveshwar Maharaj made a visit to the school. The entire school revelry honoured him with a warm greetings and garlanded welcome.

Matching with the great Indian and Hindu traditions and culture, a mass Aarti was offered to him by everybody. Everybody offered a great respect and honour to him with performing a full prostration and distribution of Prasad (sweets). He was very knowledgeable in Hindu scriptures and traditions. Vishveshwar Maharaj was highly spiritual and attentive. In a bide to showcase his prowess in knowing the past, present and future of any person, he disclosed many secretes of the employees, teachers and others during his public address that impressed everyone present in the welcome function.

After few moments, in total disrespect and disregard to the emotions and feelings of the entire school people and invited guests, Vishveshwar Maharaj kicked the plate in which the aarti-lamps were lit-up, this very much enraged me and others present, thus I took a strong objection to it and suddenly the atmosphere changed from a pious to tension filled with hurting of religious sentiments of all. The children started crying and sobbing and teachers attempted to pacify my anger generated from the displeasing incident.

Suddenly from the back-stage, Mr. Kaushik Mehta began singing the famous song, "Aprilfool Banaya...(You have been made a Fool)". It was a 1st April and thus everyone was made the fool. In fact, Vishveshwar Maharaj was nobody but in disguise he was our drawing teacher Mr. Rishi Bapodara, whom nobody could recognise. The whole plan to make the entire school as 'April Fool' was of Mr. Mehta and Mr. Bapodara.

Though, the entire school was made 'Fool', now every-year on the 1st April, we all are recalling that funny jeer and remembering Vishveshwar Majaraj and his two creators – Mr. Mehta and Mr. Bapodara. Of course, later, few senior teachers had rebuked Mr. Bapodara for '***Fooling***' them!

However, this incident also exhibits our strong feelings, emotions, respects and honours for our religions and their leaders and imminent personalities. At the same time it also exposes our weaker side and a cautioning us that how easily we could be fooled by anyone by exploiting our religious sentiments.

The 'April Fool' incident also exposes our blind faith and superstitious on our religious gurus. We have to take precautions against such weaknesses and elements!!

Visiting Schools: A Booster to My Life

In 2009, I made a visit to the London, England, to make an Educational Affiliation contract between my school and a local college. The college authority had also taken care of my hospitality by arranging accommodation in the Western London suburb.

Next day, before starting from the home, I decided to visit one of the good, reputed schools of the London, 'The Queen Elizabeth's Girls' School' which is being run by The British Royal Queen for the girls of the rich and famous families of the world. To visit this school, one mandatorily requires the prior permission from the school authority. But, unfortunately, I had not followed that mandatory protocol and necessary procedures to visit the school.

For dinner, same evening, I went to a Nepali Restaurant located just across the street of my hotel. After the dinner, I noticed an Indian couple have occupied another nearby dinner-table and to my pleasant surprise, they were talking in Gujarati! Thus, I greeted them and they also responded with equal warmth in Gujarati. Soon, we all were indulged into a good conversation, so I shifted myself over to their table.

Of the couple, the male was called Mr. Mann, Mr. Manu Patel, who was originally hailing from the Kutch region of the Gujarat. I told them my idea to visit to The Queen Elizabeth's Girls' School. To my pleasant shock and surprise, Mr Mann Patel said, "Yaar, I am The Maintenance Head of that School!" And immediately he asked me with a confident voice, "Tomorrow, what time should I pick-up you for the visit?" Indeed, next day, Mr. Patel had arranged necessary permission for me to visit the school and also an appointment with the school authority!"

Next day, I spent the entire day in the school. I visited each and every department of the school. In the History Department room, I met history teacher, Mr. Hardy, who was then watching a movie 'The Gandhi'. Mr. Hardy with a very enthusiastic voice stated, "On my home-ward journey from Japan, after spending my vacation there, I had made a short en-route-trip to India, during which I spent few days in Ahmedabad to visit the world famous 'Sabarmati Ashram' of Mahatma Gandhiji and had bought this movie 'The Gandhi'!"

"I have to take a lesson on Gandhiji tomorrow, so as a part of preparation to this, I am watching this movie," Mr. Hardy clarified.

The good schools can't be made with just infrastructural facilities, but, they require good, competent, and dedicated teachers and management to make them 'Good Schools'. Those good teachers, even during their vacation tours, make planning for their text-book lessons. The visit to the school was a pleasant surprise for me and meeting with Mr. Hardy was a wonderful experience!

My visit to any new place had a basic priority "To visit the local, good schools." And to learn new things from those visits had become ***'The Boosters for My Life!!'***

In May, 2011, I had visited The Karry Academy of North-Carolina, USA to meet Mrs. Brown who was the Dean of the school. That 45 minutes long meeting taught me many new things about the school and its management.

The school had a system to divide all the students from Std. 5 into a group of ten each. Each of these groups was being headed by a Life Advisor. This Life Advisor has had to perform role of three different personalities – A Teacher, A Inspirer, and A Psychology Expert. These Life Advisors have been entrusted with a responsibility to identify, enhance and nurture the interest, inclination and talent of each of ten students of their respective groups and to constantly encourage them to put his/her best in everything he/she is doing! The Advisor also has to keep a Live Contact with the parents of each student of his group. These Advisors will follow each student of his group for next four years. During this long and strong bond of attachment between a Guru and Disciple, the students can openly discuss and/or express their problems, difficulties, questions, and inquisitiveness with the teacher (advisor). The Advisor plays a multiple role of Father, Friend & Teacher for each student of the group.

After completion of 45-minutes long scheduled meeting, Mrs. Brown told me with a very warm and friendly tone that the further discussion and deliberation on the matter would be done through a series of email-exchanges, later, and concluded the meeting. Every Principal's desire to learn something new keeps him/her constantly agile, refresh, empowers and inspires him to do better.

The Solutions of the Problems

- ✓ With a view to improve the results of the students, a three-prong strategy was chalked out by the Management Team of the school. These three prongs were:
  - o Hard Work
  - o Constant Testing
  - o Constant Analysis

- ✓ And it took five years to improve the results from 10 % to 100%.

  To fulfill the set objective, from the very first-day an activity of group-studies was initiated in the school, it got constantly increased and gradually the school climbed up to 1st position from the ward to city level. The prestige and fame of the school started spreading in far flung areas of the city, resulting into heavy rush of the students for seeking admission into the school, that has been growing up rapidly every year. Now, every year the rush for the new-admissions is so high that over 500 students are being denied the entry.

  The school, which was opened-up with just merely 60 children few years ago, is now having over 3,500 students. Every class room is having 100% entrances!

- ✓ The school has planned out a special strategy for the last five-seven weakest students of each class to secure their success in the Board-Exams.

- ✓ Of these 5-7 weakest-students, each student will be adopted by one teacher. This teacher will visit the house of his adopted student once a week – throughout the year – to make the atmosphere of his house conducive for the study.

  Once a week, each of these students must meet me in my chamber so I can motivate him/her constantly.

  We have had planned in it such a way that every student attends the school throughout the year, till the previous day of the Board-Exams.

  We constantly attempt to motivate and energise each student, curtail their fear of exams, and to improve them in each of the mistakes they had made in the school exams.

  To achieve 100% results in the board-exams is not simply possible just with efforts. Firstly, it demands a total commitment from the Teachers and well planned management from the Principal, which descends sheer joy for everyone involved to toil very hard and finally drive them towards the fulfilment of their goal!

The Sensitivity

Once an English-Medium girl-student of 9th Standard rushed into my chamber, immediately after her third period of the History-class, and started complaining about her History-Teacher.

"Sir, our History-Teacher has twice made very vague and degrading comments on the Father of Nation, Mahatma Gandhiji in the class-room, today. I am very much upset about it. Please, you call and fire him for that mischief," she complained in just one breath and in very harsh tone.

I immediately summoned the History-Teacher into my chamber and discussed the issue with him. The teacher admitted his mistake that he had gone out of the syllabus and made comments on Gandhiji which were based on his personal thinking and ideology. He immediately went back to his history-class and rendered his apology to the whole class and admitted that his comments were based on his personal belief on Mahatma Gandhiji.

The teaching of virtues, values and making comments and/or criticism on life and deeds of the imminent and giant national leaders and heroes by the teachers in the school are often leaving deep rooted lasting impressions and impacts on the immature and innocent brains and hearts of the students. And as a result often those beliefs of the teachers become a line of thinking or ideology of the children.

Such incidents are often taking place in the class-room. The insensitivity of the teachers towards values, virtues and national heroes could often change the direction of line of thinking of the immature and innocent minds of the children. Therefore, the limits of Code-of-Conduct for the teachers should be clearly drawn and specified, so no teacher can dare to cross his limits to express his personal beliefs or mind-set while teaching to the students or at least he would think twice before doing so!

The values and virtues have been degraded in our society, particularly in recent past decades, because of the ideals and values taught in the class-room are having very lesser or none implementation in reality in the society and the school as well. Thus, often the child accepts the thought-process that there can be a contradiction between saying and doing. As an ultimate result of these, our faith and confidence in our system, law and judiciary and national character have been diminishing day-by-day!

Hero to Zero

Once, I accidentally entered into the Kindergarten class-room of the Gujarati-Medium and I asked the child seated on the first bench to read the sentences written above each picture of the book he was holding.

In the book, above the first picture the sentence written was "My Father", but to my surprise and shock, the child read it as "Ajay's Father", "Ajay's Mummy", "Ajay's Home"...! On each page, the child was replacing 'My' with 'Ajay's'.

The teacher explained that the child was reading like that because the book was of Ajay who was seated next to him!

The minds of the children are very sensitive and receptive about the fantasy and reality, thus, often when you tell them the stories or fairytales they get so much engrossed into them like they are really a part of them and real world!

Rather than enhancing and expanding his power of fantasy and imagination further with proper usage of his sensitivity and sensuality, we are grounding him through puzzling and baffling his mind in the triangle of questions, answers, and marks then ultimately converting him from a highly imaginative human to a 'Money Earning' robot!

That is why, the famous Mr. J. Krishnamurthy has said, "Child's 70% inspirations are being shattered and battered during his schooling years and rest by the parents at home and by the society in the world!"

First we make a person 'Zero' and then searching a 'Hero' within him!

The Society's entire lot of insensitive people, is a production lot of yester-years' class-room!!

The Saturday Morning

Every Saturday the academic activity is beginning at 08:00 a.m. in our school, but, the teachers are arriving at 07:00 a.m. to attend a customary weekly meeting.

This one-hour long customary weekly meeting being held between 07:00-08:00 am every Saturday is holding the real key to our success!

At these Saturday meetings, we are chalking out our micro-level planning for the events going to be held in next seven-days at school. This planning also includes pin-pointing the responsibility for allotted works and issuance of the directives. At the meetings it was also being discussed about the events that have had happened in the last seven days at the school. If there is no significant agenda needed to be discussed at the meeting than 'English Improvement Tutorial' lectures are being delivered to the teachers with an aim to teach and improve their English Grammar skill.

Mr. Rajendrasinh Shinole, a successful teacher of our school, was entrusted with a responsibility to write minutes on every agenda discussed at the weekly meetings, and those minutes must be signed by the attended teachers. These minutes are so much informative and interesting that there collection can be released as a Book. The way Mr. Shinole has taken care in writing the minutes books with sincerity and precision for last seven-year, is simply deserving the praise. Mr. Shinole possesses a deep rooted curiosity, enthusiasm and sensitivity for his works and duties that makes him a jewel for the school.

Every week we are planning with the teachers on 'How to do better at every aspect in the school?"

I strongly believe that for the success of the school, meetings with the constructive and innovative ideas should be held between the teachers and the principal on regular schedule. These meetings definitely, distinctively benefiting the school; and the Principal should be more prepared to adopt and implement those constructive and innovative ideas.

The programmes organised like this in some schools, can be inspirational for many others. I had also derived the inspiration similarly from somewhere to begin this, which has given many wonderful results.

The status and position of the school principal is as such that everything depends on him. If he desires, there is 'NO WORK' in the school which he must do himself, and if he desires he can always find himself 'NOT FREE' for a minute. In fact, he himself has to decided about it from his self-consciousness that what he compensate for the Rs 1,000/- being paid everyday by the Government to him.

The Effect of Training

Our school has a tradition to conduct 'The Yearly Training Programme' for the entire teaching staff from June 1 to 10. During this ten-day long Training Programme, the teaching staff members undergo a vigorous training on various new concepts and ideas in teachings at the school level. This Training Programme is at the core of the rapid and vast growth of the school. The school management is organizing this training programme very carefully and allocating a whooping budget of Rs 1-Lac for it. The Management is also selecting the training modules for the programme. This Training programme has few focal points such as:

- ✓ Selection of the Monitors and deliberation on its results
- ✓ Few teachers opined to favour selection rather than election of the Monitors, thus, a detail discussion was held on the issue.
- ✓ Normally the boy, who has an image to be the naughtiest and strongest boy of the class, gets selected as the monitor!
- ✓ The Monitor controls the class-room, mostly in the absence of the teacher, and enjoys the power of being a half-a-teacher.
- ✓ Normally the Monitor is the one who has a very strong image on the minds of rest of students of the class and none can challenge his superiority.

- ✓ Other naughty students of the class feel that to become a Monitor, they must become much stronger and must form a gang against the present Monitor.
- ✓ The bright, sincere and mild natured students refrained themselves from becoming the Monitor and believe that the Monitor is a Nuisance appreciation of the class.
- ✓ The results of the deliberation was that:
- ✓ Today's political scenario is a mirror image or result of yesterday's class-room scene. A good, disciplined citizen who avoids the politics is the same student of the yester-years, who was shut-upped by the naughtiest student (Monitor).
- ✓ Our messed-up and dirty political scenario is an outcome of yester-years' class-room. Thus, the remedy to this scenario has to be initiated from the class-room level.
- ✓ Training Modules conducted in the class-room are very effective and they are chosen very carefully with the class-room situation taken into consideration. Some of the technologies, concepts and ideas of the modules get implemented in the class-room.
- ✓ Various Teaching Methods.
- ✓ Effective Parenting.
- ✓ A special focus on weaker students to improve them.
- ✓ Effective Teaching.
- ✓ Physical Punishment is a cognizable crime.
- ✓ A Code of Conduct for the Teacher.
- ✓ A success of the class-teacher.

- ✓ Every child of the class-room possesses the Godly existence.
- ✓ Positive Attitude.
- ✓ The School Principal is submitting a report to the School Trustee that what new teaching techniques and methods the teachers have learnt through the Training Programme. And they also discuss about the academic progress of the school.

Training: A Necessity

For a successful management of any educational institute, the training is an essential and inevitable element at every level -- ranging from Peon–Principal--Trustee! It is necessary to make a deliberation on the results of the Training:

Training and its results:

- ✓ It changes the person's attitude and approach
- ✓ It changes the person's perception
- ✓ It widens the purview of the person
- ✓ It changes the solutions of the questions
- ✓ It changes the path of the development
- ✓ It redefines the definition of the resources
- ✓ It enhances the capacity of the employee
- ✓ It changes the growth of the institution
- ✓ It makes the success a reality
- ✓ It eradicates the limitations
- ✓ It brings changes, develops interest and inclination in the works
- ✓ It connects the hands and the head with the heart
- ✓ It gives a vision to recognize and solve the problems

"The money spent on the training programmes, is an investment": this vision is possible only when the institute's top management – ***which is the Eye, Ear, & Brain*** – has an attitude to adopt the fresh ideas, concepts, techniques and technologies.

When, a Chief Trustee or Principal of a school loses his confidence in the training, then he loses confidence in the reforms. The one, who loses confidence in the reforms, also looses the confidence in the developmental too!

That is why I am a strong advocator of the Training Programme! As a result of this mind-set, even after vast experience of 30 years' in the school education, I am always willing to learn a few new tricks and things of the trade every day in the rapidly changing scenario of the teaching world.

I would like to express, "The results of the Training I have experienced".

Teaching Values:

To impart the 'Teaching Values' in the students of the D. P. School, we have had conducted a pilot project under the able guidance of Rajyogini Chandrika Didi, the founder of the Mahadev Nagar Centre of world renowned The Brahmakumris Vishvadihyalaya, in year 2004. As a consequence positive result of this project, the Brahmakumaris Institution is conducting 'Teaching Value' programme at over 2000 schools spreads over width and breadth of the India. Through this programme the fame and name of the D. P. School has also spread in almost every nook and corner of the country. And I am very proud on everyone who is involved in the success of this programme.

This is a real life model that proves: ***"A Reform is Possible through Training!"***

The Shackle of Inferiority Complex

When a baby-elephant is shackled down with a strong-rope at the tender age for the first time, initially it tries very hard to set itself free with its best efforts and when it fails, it develops a psychological inferiority complex in its mind that ***"I would never succeed in freeing myself from the shackling of this strong rope"*** and thus, finally it gives up the idea of FREEDOM. This psychological barrier continues to hound it even at the younger-age too when in fact the baby-elephant has groomed itself into very strong young-elephant and now it is very easy to set itself free, but, his mind continues to make him believe that he can't free itself!!. The seed of the inferiority complex sowed in the mind of baby-elephant at very tender age never let it realize its real power and strength thus his brain never issues a command to unshackle the chain it is tied with!

Same way, when the parents often give discouraging instructions to the child such as 'You can't do that', 'you are not capable to do this or that', as results of these unfortunate behaviour knowingly or unknowingly they are developing an inferiority complex in the tender and immature mind of the child. Thus, just like the baby-elephant, the child also stops to make attempts to break-open the shackle though he is very strong young-man now!

A Letter from 9th Std. Student of the School

Respected, Mr. Jaydevsinh Sir,

We're privileged to studying in a school that is not just imparting educational knowledge and teachings on to us, but, rendering all sort of directives such as General-knowledge, Sports, along with teaching of the subjects such as Science and Mathematics. I am so much overwhelm with the emotions flowing in my heart that I am not able to decide how could I offer my 'Vote of Thanks' to you and our esteemed institute. The directives imparted upon us by you for living life in happiness, enthusiasm and merrily have made us capable to find-out the right solution in any difficult times. Any mammoth and difficult task becomes an easy for us because of the guidance and directives you have taught us.

Our school's visit to the Science City on 18th December, 2008 was really very educative and informative as well for us. The visit taught us the usage of science in many ways in daily life, particularly various usages of the Solar Energy in instruments like Solar Water Heater, Solar Cooker, and Solar House and so on...!! The visit to the Solar House was simply an unforgettable experience of the life time. Then we visited the Plastic House. It was simply unimaginable to realize that every utility made in the Plastic House were made of the Plastic and surprisingly the used Plastic was completely harmless to the environment and society, contrary to the general belief! And then later visits made to the Hall of Space & Hall of Science were also very educative and informative, including the screenings of the movies 'Planet Marsh' and 'Effects of Global Warming.' We all had thoroughly enjoyed both the films. The movies had narrated very vividly the causes generating natural calamities such as floods, earthquakes, and others. They also educated us on how to prevent their happenings and how to save self and others when such things are occurring.

The Manager of the Science City made all of us to take a pledge that "Daily, we all will plant a tree and to save energy in day-to-day usages and we all enjoyed his guidance and treatment he offered to us during the visit.

Thanks Sir,

Yours faithfully,
Student of Std. 9th 'B'.

The Quotations on Parenting

1. To become a Mother-Father is an incident, but, to become the parent of a baby is an uphill task as it demands a constant perseverance for growing-up the baby in the correct perception.
2. The parents with a vision to foresee the future-life of their baby for next 25-years are mostly capable to take the right decisions for their child.
3. The children are the keys to make the family life heavenly.
4. The best gift you can give to your children is neither money nor amenities, but, your invaluable time.
5. The decision to make the baby means to give a new shape to the hearts of the mother and father and combine their emotions in the form of a new-baby.
6. A deeply sleeping baby has right to get a sequel of softer kisses from her dear and near ones, particularly from the parents. Please don't take-away this right.
7. For a mother bringing-up a baby is like a tale narrated with the tears of happiness.
8. For a woman attaining of mother-hood is like taking third-birth and then dedicating the entire life for it.
9. At my marriage time I had four wonderful ideas on "How to raise a baby?", now, I have four children but can't recall those ideas!
10. We must see our children like our role-model, not like super model. Please check yourself!

11. A baby needs your presence, not your presents!
12. No need to take precaution about that the child doesn't over-heard you, but, you must be careful as the baby will always be watching you.
13. To become a good parent to your child means to get prepared to become his gentleman enemy.
14. The children are the base to grow older, not the support for the old-age.
15. Don't make your child cripple or dependable by offering him/her all amenities, as life is a ***STRUGGLE.***
16. Just by giving a birth to child doesn't mean you have achieved the parenthood, in fact, you have just become mother.
17. The child is not a device to fulfil your expectations and uncompleted dreams, but, surely it could be a medium.
18. The first-child draws 100% attention of the mother, but, the second-child grows up on his owns, so mostly second-child will be mentally stronger.
19. By not obeying to the parents, the children are testing parents' capacity to understand, and scaling the levels of tolerance and gentleness.
20. When grown-up the children are paying back everything to the parents what they have received during the childhood.
21. If a child is shying or hiding away from you then consider this act of his as you might be lacking of something.
22. The wrong growing up is at the root cause of every problem being faced by the society, which needs to be improved.
23. The world is a stage and each of us are the artist to play our character, thus, the child who has grown

up holding the finger of his parents, become the supporter to the same hand in their old-age.

24. Growing up a child is like teaching him how to ride a bicycle... holding, leaving...then again holding, leaving...and finally leaving him to set free on his path of destiny.
25. The children are like stone-balls; always keeping you in doubts and guesses– to eat/not to eat, ultimately troublesome.
26. When a baby born, she is like a wonderful flower. At school-age, she is like a tennis-ball. But, at teenage, it becomes leather-ball and then it becomes very difficult to play!
27. Amongst the all living beings on the earth, the human is the only species that tries to hold its baby forever.
28. The child adapts mother and teacher faster than the shoes.
29. The parenting is like a voyage where every mile-stone has a different meaning and path continues to grow further than never ending.
30. It is easy to be the parents, but, very hard to come-out of it.
31. The parents are often sending the children to summer-camp to take break from their responsibility.
32. Parenting is not a liability.
33. The God is still sending children on earth, means He has a confidence that the world is going to survive.
34. The biggest problem of the parenting is that by the time you have learnt everything, the task of the parenting gets over; and your children don't require your advices and counselling because just like you, they also want to experience everything on their own in the life!

35. The time you have spent for and with the kids gives better returns than the money you have spent on them.
36. When the parent fight with each other for the custody or attention of the child, then the child enjoys his/her freedom from the parents.
37. The arrival of the child brings dreams and hopes for the parents, but, in fact, he/she poses a bundle of problems for them and take away their important and large chunk of vital period of the lives.
38. The Almighty has created the child for the better coordination of the time amongst the humans, so they don't spend time on the negative activities.
39. The parents visit every temple and shrine to receive blessing of the Almighty to have their own baby, though the same baby sends them to old-age-house at the fag-end of their life yet they continue to wish the good for him. This proves that yet humanity is still alive.
40. The parenting is like a festival. But you have to decide: Holi or Deepawali.
41. Even after divorce the parent continue to fight over the custody of the children. **The parenting is a Partnership Firm and the children are the documents of an agreement that cannot be divided.**
42. Initially mother and father are encouraging the child to learn quickly: "How to speak" and later attempt very hard to keep his mouth shut. Then, how could a child observes a mum?
43. Often children influence the emotions and feelings (love) of the parents and then leave them alone to walk away on their own paths of life.

44. The only task that human does with the total integrity is raising their kids. In this task honesty is totally truthful but method is always wrong.
45. A guide on how to raise a child is easily available but the understanding is changing from human-to-human.
46. The mother of a naughty child feels relaxed when he falls to sleep.
47. The parenting is a THANKLESS job; that gives satisfaction but award cannot be won.
48. I have found a very few fathers who enjoy refuge and relaxation in the family-life.
49. The raising of the children is an adventure, of course it is inevitable. However, finally it gives you feelings of a misadventure.
50. For you every dawn is like a blank canvas. You draw a new picture and then colour it too. So why to remorse then?
51. Every encampment of human-life offers an opportunity for adventurism to youth, shelter to handicapped, and reasons to smile for the children, so let everyone live!
52. The parents spend most of their time in worrying over how and which way their children are grooming and rest of the time they spend in cross-checking whether the children have had groomed correctly or not.
53. The parents having 'No-faith' in the capability of their children are amassing the huge wealth with a view to secure their future.
54. Just like as you check-out your bank balance at the regular intervals, similarly the children are also

constantly monitoring mother and father to check-out is there any decrease in their love for them.

55. If the schools were not made, then the majority of the mothers would have been living in the rehabilitation-centres and fathers in the forests!!
56. A child is like a promissory-note, not a bearer cheque, thus you must preserve till the date of maturity.
57. The guidance-books on parenting are easily available, but courage and fortune you must create on your own.
58. It is better to bind the children with the bondage of love and care rather than fear and pressure. The former virtues will keep them bounded.
59. A child is symbol of freedom, a customer to slavery, a citizen of monarchy, a death to dictatorship, and sometimes creates illusion. Whatever he is, he is a symbol of your system!
60. A child is an ancestor of the family, an ideal of system, mirror of the home, a real form of the Self. He is a mirror to your face.
61. A child is a treasure of happiness, an indicator of cyclone, a stream of love, and a wave of energy. You have to sail with it, so be prepared.
62. A child is a bundle of a problem. It is up to you to open it or not!
63. A child is not like a '**TEDDY-BEAR**' who can be made thin and thick as per desire. In fact, you must learn to love it, whatever it is!
64. In half of the efforts the parents can adjust themselves to the child than their efforts to make the child adjustable to them.

65. To change a child is an uphill task, while it is easier to change the self.
66. It is not true that today's children are not like the previous generations, but, in fact, it is the parents who have not yet changed their vision to understand the children.
67. When a question is pertaining to the entire society, then, it is not a problem, but a situation in which you have to get adjusted, it cannot be challenged.
68. It would be a better experience, if a teacher tries to be a trainer rather than the director.
69. Today's education system is turning a child in to a money-making machine and is squeezing his emotions.
70. Today's education system is largely based on 'Securing of Marks in Exams'. It has inter-linked ***KNOWLEDGE*** and ***GROWTH*** with each other.
71. In present day's education system we have forgotten the months and seasons such as summer, winter, spring, and monsoon and only remembering months of exams.
72. Admitting a child in the school lacking of activities, means putting him/her into a imprisonment of four-walls, where the development and growth has the one meaning.
73. Compared to the teacher, the new generation students are lagging behind in study by just 45 minutes but ahead in understanding by ten-years.
74. In tandem with the parents, the school can put toiling efforts for the conclusive development of the child. But, for that the parents must come to the school!

75. The parenting doesn't mean to keep a watch on child's 'Progress Report', but, to understand his 'Progress'.
76. "My child is weak in the Maths, please take care of him/her," this kind of instructive notes from the parents to the class-teacher or subject-teacher, are not simply disclosing the lack of ability of the child, but also weakness of the parents!
77. The children found weaker in calculating sums of mathematics in the school years, are mostly found very precise in the calculating mathematics of the 'LIFE'!!
78. For imparting education don't differentiate between a girl or boy child; higher the child is educated and cultured, more he/she will pluck the fruits.
79. I think, down the line after 50-years, the parents will be sending the children to the school for 24x7 and will ask for a permission to meet him/her/them for 10 minutes for an exchange of hugs and kisses.
80. To make the class-room like a heaven, the teacher must behave like a parent.
81. To make the naughtiest student of the class as a 'Monitor' means to create another 'Lallu Yadav' of tomorrow!
82. The True teacher is that who pick-up the last-bencher student and make him a brilliant one.
83. At least, make the child capable enough so that he can use the wealth in proper manner for whom, you have amassed the wealth.
84. A naughty child is like a car without breaks that can be speed-up but cannot be halted at the right moment.

85. A successful father is that who can be childlike with the children.
86. A healthy home is that where the books are housing and the family members are reading them!
87. For a child, the home without grand-parents is like he is deprived of his childhood.
88. The home is not a guest-house where you could raise your demands, but, in fact, it is housing emotions and love of your dear and near ones.
89. The home is not shining-out by availability of facilities, amenities, furniture & furnishings, but, by the culture, nature and emotions of the persons living in it.
90. Those who don't have time for the children, in time they also loose their children too.
91. They are mistaken who believes that '***Money is everything,***' the money can bring degrees and education, but, not success.
92. The ***BIRTH*** is an accident, the ***NURTURING*** is cooperation, and the ***SUCCESS*** is an experiment, nothing more than that.
93. We need to understand and realise that the root cause of diminishing of humanity in today's adults is lying in the vanishing of their childhood at child-age.
94. Most mothers and fathers are living between the past and present times, while very few are breathing in the prevalent era.
95. The child is a subtle cause to create quarrel between the husband and wife, but, at the same time the child is a bridge to connect love between them.
96. I am still able to vividly recall the naughty incidents and memories of the childhood, however, of course

not able to remember remorse for lacking of toys, sweets, and so on.

97. I am not able to derive the same sort of happiness and pleasures from the ample facilities and money I possessed today, compared to the joy and excitements I am availing by recalling the wonderful memories and times of my childhood.
98. Till date I am vibrantly remembering my geography teacher, Mr. N. B. Patel because every time he was coming to the class-room to take his geography lecture he was always carrying maps and charts with him like they are undivided parts of existence.
99. In my memoir past, I am still remembering more of my childhood-pals than friends of my college days.
100. A lecture from any of the orators of the world could not ever impressed me as much as I have been by my primary teacher, Mr. Ratilal Nayak whenever he was singing song 'Dada ho Dikri".
101. My growth is nothing but a education-hunger of my mother and father.
102. Our childhood habits to hear and sing songs in the house have played a key-role in making us good orators, writers and successful human beings.
103. It is important to give an opportunity to the child that sowing a seed for the development of his personality.

About the Author

Mr. Jaydevsinh Sonagara hails from Bolundra (Sonagara) village of Idar taluka in Sabarkantha district. He has studied M.A, B.Ed. with English literature.

His fruitful visits to premier institutes in about ten countries have helped him to gain vast knowledge and acquaintance with the latest happenings in the teaching field.

His elder son Mr. Vishvajit Sonagara has been working as a software engineer in a leading finance company in USA. His younger son Mr Abhijit sonagara has been associated with many educational institutions and also running a branding company – ADOZ. His wife Mrs. Janakben Sonagara, who had just studied up to a metric at the time of marriage, is now a graduate and largely lends creative contributions in the school management.

Mr. Sonagara's journey from a humble farmer's son to a successful director of the renowned educational institutes has been a progressive, developmental and inspirational odyssey.

❖ As many as four schools are running under his headship:

- D. P. High School, Nava Wadaj, Principal and Trustee
- Divyapah Campus, Memnagar, Managing Trustee
- Nest Public School, Ranip, Trustee
- S.G.V.P. International School, Director

The first three schools in above list have witnessed 100% success from scratch.

Owing to his interest in all-round growths of children, he has dig deep in the areas like writing, research and parenting, and guided over 50,000 parents so far on successful upbringing of their kids. As a versatile talent, he has also penned about 50 poems and wrote effectively on more than 250 debate topics.

A sensible human being, he could fathom children's unspoken afflictions within four walls of classroom, and could guide his students in leading a skillful life instead of getting stuck in rat race.

More than 5,000 students studied under his able guidance have made successful career as doctors, engineers, officers and industrialists.

His guidance has proved a philosopher's stone which has transformed many ordinary children into successful speakers and journalists.

His institutions have made a sort of revolution by making education a fun, thanks to his keenness in learning new things and his faith in training.

In 2011, Mr. Sonagara made paper presentation before 600 principals of educational institutes across the world on "Effective Solution of School Problems" at IIT Delhi. He also visited two leading schools of America, gave training to 500 teachers and did parenting programme for over 7,000 parents.

Rajendra Shinol
D. P. High School

I take this opportunity to express my heartiest thankfulness to following people for giving words to my thoughts, ideas and experiences.

Mrs. Janak J. Sonagara,
Mrs. Vedika V. Sonagara,
Mr. Vishvajit J. Sonagara,
Mr. Abhijit Sonagara,
Mr. Rajendrasinh Shilon,
Mr. Shashikant Vaghela,
Mrs. Mansi Chandel, my school staff, friends and well wishers.

****

This book

- Has a divine path for an all-round growth of children.
- Gives divine insight into directing children.
- Has 'Sure Success' formula for child rearing.
- Turns child's failure into success.
- Uncovers bright future for children.
- Gives expressions to children's emotions.
- Has divine magical power to bring happiness into the family.

:Divyapath Family

The parents wishing to nurture children's life on right path must read this book; must make self-deliberation; and outcome of the self-deliberation must be implemented:

Swami Madhavpriyadasji,
Shree Swaminarayan Gurukul, SGVP,
Chharodi.

The book will entirely change the beliefs and attitudes of the parents, thus, will transform the bright future for children too!: Dr. Ashok Patel, Educationist, Ahmedabad.

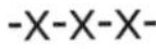

'Nurturing' is an important process of the life. Through this book, Mr. Jaydevsinh Sonagara has beautifully presented many interesting aspects of child rearing and that too that they can be very helpful to the parents: Dr Prashant Bhimani, Consulting Psychologist and Hypnotherapist.

-x-x-x-